英文版 東京B級グルメガイド

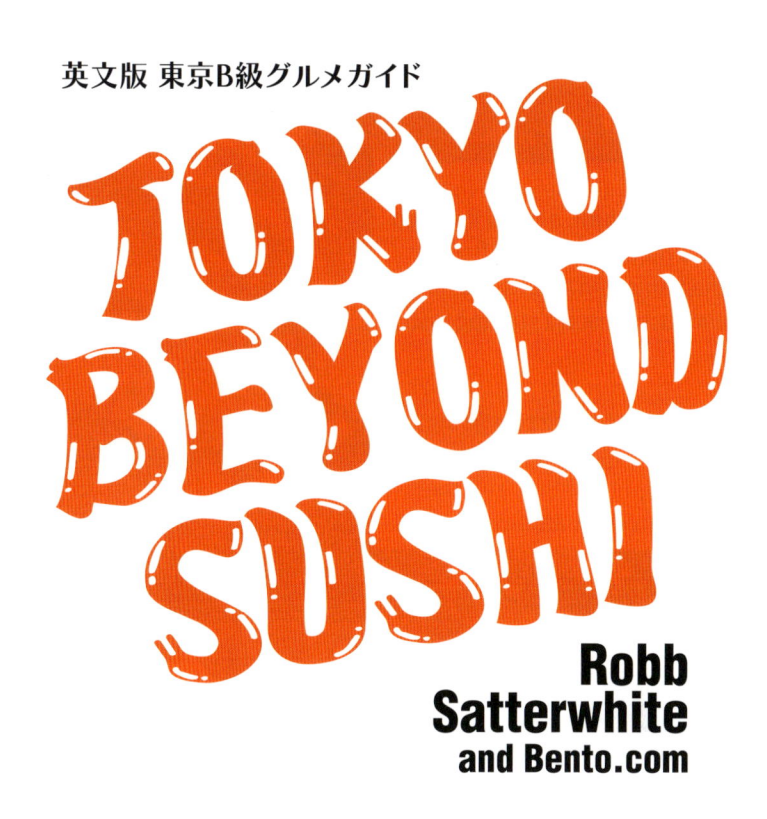

TOKYO BEYOND SUSHI

**Robb Satterwhite
and Bento.com**

IBCパブリッシング

Yakiton is grilled pork on skewers, often served in very informal after-work drinking spots along with beer and sake.

Motsu-nikomi, a richly flavored stew made from pork, beef or chicken organ meats, is a quick and tasty izakaya starting dish.

The best **yakitori** shops take pride in their premium heirloom-breed chickens, the skills of their grill masters, and the quality of the charcoal that they use.

Horse meat is a local favorite in several different regions of Japan, served grilled, in stews or raw as sashimi or sushi.

Grilled **beef tongue**, a favorite local dish of the Sendai area, can be found in a growing number of Tokyo specialty shops.

Part of the enjoyment of deep-fried **kushiage** skewers is the surprise of discovering what's underneath the breading.

Crisp **sara udon** noodles with seafood and vegetables are a local specialty from Kyushu's Nagasaki region.

The subtle flavors of simmered fish cakes and other **oden** ingredients go well with delicate sake.

A crunchy deep-fried shell and tender, succulent meat are the hallmarks of a well-prepared **tonkatsu** pork cutlet.

Deep-fried **gyukatsu** (beef cutlet), rare in the middle and served with wasabi, is one of Tokyo's newest food trends.

A long-time favorite of foreign visitors, savory **okonomiyaki** pancakes provide a good balance of seafood, pork and vegetables.

One of the attractions of **curry udon** is the ability to customize your bowl with a variety of extra ingredients.

Houtou noodles are a hearty wintertime dish from the mountainous Kofu area (ninety minutes west of Tokyo).

Many of Tokyo's **ramen** shops are culinary laboratories where chefs experiment with new flavors.

Curry rice is Japan's best loved comfort food, with its own unique character and history.

The simple **Hamburg steak**, made from ground beef and/or pork, is a staple of retro-style yoshoku cuisine.

The **fried-rice omelette**, an adaptation of European cuisine from the early twentieth century, has a nostalgic appeal to modern Tokyo diners.

Hayashi rice, with beef and onions in a rich gravy, is another old-fashioned European-style dish with a long history.

A uniquely Japanese take on Italian pasta, **wafu spaghetti** incorporates ingredients like spicy cod roe, sea urchin, shiso leaves and toasted seaweed.

Tokyo's best burger chefs are very serious about the art of the gourmet **hamburger**, and produce some excellent results.

As is fitting for a cosmopolitan city, Tokyo's culinary scene draws on international influences, including **exotic sandwiches** from around the world.

Deep-fried pork-filled **gyoza** dumplings have evolved from their Chinese origins to develop their own unique character.

Takoyaki (octopus dumplings) are a beloved local dish from the Osaka area.

Akashiyaki are a regional variation of takoyaki (octopus dumplings) made with a more eggy batter.

You can find it everywhere from cafeterias to convenience stores, but some of the best **karaage** (fried chicken) comes from shops that specialize in this one dish.

Not just a summertime dish, **kakigori** (shaved ice) in exotic and creative flavors draws fans year-round.

Tasty food to take home is sold in department store food halls, restaurant-operated food stalls, and local prefectural shops all over Tokyo.

Introducing Japan's comfort foods and everyday cuisines

What this book is all about
There's much more to Japanese food than just sushi and Kobe beef, and the goal of this book is to introduce the other 95% of Japanese cuisine to food lovers from around the world.

Foreign visitors to Tokyo, even sophisticated gourmets and experienced world diners, often have preconceived ideas about how to eat here. Many enthusiastic self-styled foodies want to find the "best sushi in Tokyo" and eat it three times a day, while other more adventurous diners might be willing to alternate super-expensive sushi with exorbitantly priced steaks, always made from the finest Kobe beef, of course.

Tokyo's sushi and beef restaurants are very good, of course, but there's a whole other world of fantastic food that gourmet visitors tend to miss out on, usually without even knowing it. In particular, there are dozens of humble-seeming, often inexpensive everyday dishes that are beloved and sought out by Tokyoites who love good food.

What is B-kyu cuisine?
In Japanese, these simple, very popular foods enjoyed on an everyday basis—pork cutlet, savory okonomiyaki pancakes, curry rice and many more—are often referred to as "B-kyu" cuisine. The term is very tongue-in-cheek, as "B-kyu" simply means "B-grade," as in B-grade

movies—not intellectual art films but fun monster movies that anyone can enjoy.

B-kyu cuisine, then, is the culinary equivalent of comfort food rather than high gastronomy, and the B-kyu gourmet is someone who can appreciate the subtle charms of the perfectly fried pork cutlet or the painstakingly prepared ramen soup, and will seek out the best of these creations. In this book I will attempt to introduce some of Japan's favorite B-kyu cuisines, along with the Tokyo shops that have turned these humble dishes into works of art.

Some of these foods, like curry rice and gyoza dumplings, superficially resemble foreign dishes, but have evolved their own unique identities in Japan. Other cuisines, like ramen noodles, are becoming better known abroad, but are much more varied in style and generally better in quality than you can find outside Japan. A few of them, like Japanese-style wafu spaghetti, might appeal to adventurous diners with broad tastes, while others, like deep-fried chicken karaage, should be instant crowd pleasers.

How the restaurants were selected

In a city like Tokyo with more than 100,000 restaurants, it would be an endless and impossible task trying to determine the "best" tonkatsu or curry or grilled pork in town. And over the years I've visited some highly rated shops that may serve an excellent version of whatever their specialty might be, but otherwise offer a less-than-fun dining experience, with austere decor, minimal drinks options, harsh lighting and overall lack of amenities and atmosphere.

For this book, then, I've tried to recommend places that I personally like to visit, restaurants that balance excellent food with the many other factors that make for an enjoyable meal. These include lively atmosphere and friendly service, pleasant decor, good sake and other drinks, reasonably easy access from central Tokyo, and good value for money. Extra points go to places with non-smoking areas, tables and chairs as well as tatami floor seating, and credit-card terminals.

While it's always fun to discover some obscure mom-and-pop place that only seats twelve people and has been using the same stew pot for fifty years, I've also recommended well-run chain restaurants when they provide great food and good value. Also, some of my favorite restaurants in Tokyo are located in shopping complexes and office-building basements—that's simply where regular people go to eat. In general I've tried to recommend a range of prices and dining styles, with a mix of old-school traditional shops and newer, more modern approaches to the same cuisines.

For the ramen and kakigori (shaved ice) chapters of the book, I have entrusted selection and reviews of the shops to ramen expert Brian MacDuckston, who runs the well-known ramen blog "Ramen Adventures" and is the author of the bilingual ramen guidebook *Brian's Ramen Adventures* (2015 K&B Publishers). (He is also the Ramen Editor at Bento.com.)

Rules for dining in izakaya-style restaurants

The first section of the book covers cuisines and dishes that are often found in izakaya-style restaurants (drinking spots that serve food, or pubs), and many of the recommended venues are izakayas. When you dine at an izakaya in the evening, there are two basic rules that it's important to know about. (Note that these rules apply in the evening, not at lunchtime.)

- Order at least one drink, and order it first, before ordering food.
- You will receive a tiny dish of food to go with your drink, and you will be charged for it.

Neither of these is optional—the economics of running an izakaya are built around these two rules. If you don't want to drink alcohol, then order an iced oolong tea ('uroncha'). If you don't want to eat the tiny dish of food that comes with your food (it's called an 'otoshi'), just leave it on the table, don't attempt to send it back to the kitchen. The charge for the otoshi is equivalent to a table charge; it's usually not that expensive—¥300–500 is typical—and you get some food for your money. Basically izakaya consider themselves to be drinking spots rather than restaurants, even though they may serve a wide assortment of food, which is why they will take your drink order as soon as you sit down.

If an izakaya has a raised tatami-mat section, you will be expected to take off your shoes before entering that area. If you need to use the hygienic facilities during the course of your meal, slippers will be provided for your journey to the toilet, and separate slippers may or may not be provided in the toilet area.

Most izakaya and other restaurants will leave a check on your table when you've gotten all the food you've ordered, but sometimes you need to ask for the check. Usually you take the check up to the cash register at the front of the shop rather than paying at your table. Oh, and note that many shops that serve B-kyu cuisine take cash only, no credit cards, so be prepared.

Contents

Chapter 1 Izakaya-style pub fare 居酒屋メニュー

Yakiton (grilled pork), Motsu nikomi (stews) やきとん、もつ煮込み ·· 16
Yakitori (grilled chicken) 焼き鳥 ································· 30
Beef tongue and more meat dishes 牛タン、他の肉料理 ···· 44
Kushiage (deep-fried skewers) 串揚げ ···························· 56
Oden (fish cakes in broth) おでん ································· 66
Regional dishes and other comfort foods ご当地グルメ ····· 76

Chapter 2 Budget meals お手頃メニュー

Tonkatsu (pork cutlet) 豚カツ ····································· 86
Gyūkatsu (beef cutlet) 牛カツ ····································· 96
Okonomiyaki and Monjayaki (savory pancakes)
　お好み焼き、もんじゃ焼き ·· 104
Udon (wheat noodles) and Curry udon うどん、カレーうどん ·· 114
Rāmen ラーメン ··· 124

Chapter 3 International influences 日本流

Japanese curry カレーライス ····································· 146
Yōshoku (retro-style European dishes) レトロな洋食 ········ 158
Wafū (Japanese-style) spaghetti 和風スパゲティー ·········· 170
Burgers ハンバーガー ··· 178
Exotic sandwiches サンドイッチのニューウエーブ ············ 186

Chapter 4 Casual and takeaway
　　　　　　　　　　　軽食・お持ち帰りもできます

Gyōza (pork dumplings) 餃子 ···································· 196
Takoyaki and Akashiyaki (octopus dumplings)
　たこ焼き、明石焼き ··· 204
Chicken karaage (deep-fried chicken) 鶏の唐揚げ ············ 214
Kakigōri (shaved-ice desserts) カキ氷 ························· 222
Regional "antenna shops" and more takeaway
　地方特産品アンテナショップ ·································· 228

13

装幀:岩目地英樹(コムデザイン)
デザイン・DTP:ギルド
撮影:Robb Satterwhite

Chapter 1

Izakaya-style pub fare

居酒屋メニュー

Online Map
bento.com/maps/pubs.html

Yakiton, Motsu nikomi

(grilled pork, stews)

やきとん、もつ煮込み

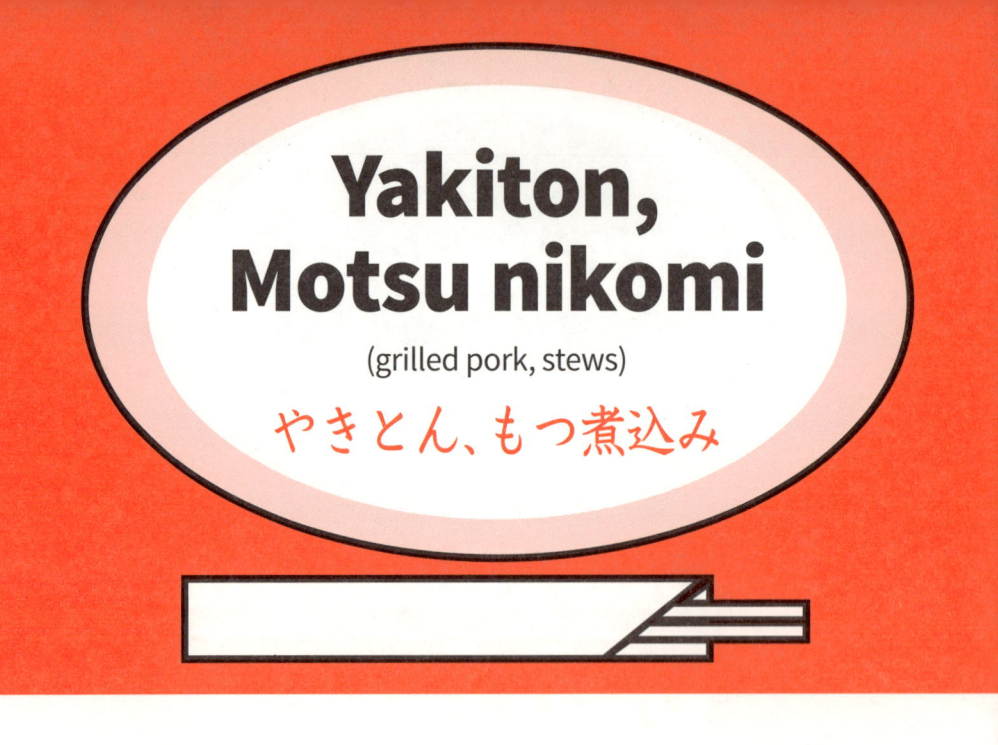

Yakiton is simply grilled pork on skewers, the porcine version of yakitori (grilled chicken). But while you can find fancy, upscale yakitori shops with stylish decor and nice wines, most yakiton specialists are cheap and casual. There's also an emphasis on organ meats such as liver, tongue, stomach and shiro (intestines) in addition to meatier cuts.

As with yakitori, you'll usually be given a choice of having your meat basted in sauce (tare) or simply sprinkled with salt (shio) before grilling. Grilled skewers often come with either yuzu-kosho (a spicy citrus-red pepper paste) or mustard on the side. You can also add powdered red pepper that's supplied on your table or counter.

Buta motsu nikomi (pork organ-meat stew) is a staple side dish at places that serve yakiton. "Motsu" refers to organ meats, and motsu nikomi is a rich stew made by slowly simmering these meats in a thick broth, often miso-based.

It tends to be a hearty dish with deep flavors well suited to accompanying sake, shochu, beer or wine.

Motsu nikomi can be made from beef and chicken organ meats as well as pork, and **gyu (beef) Motsu nikomi** in particular is a traditional izakaya dish with a long history. Some Tokyo izakaya that are famous for their nikomi have been in business for fifty to a hundred years, maintaining their secret recipes through the decades.

Because they're so informal, izakaya that offer motsu nikomi and yakiton are usually quite comfortable for solo visitors or small groups to drop into for a quick drink and snack. They do vary somewhat in style—you can find lively after-work standing bars, more cozy traditional drinking spots with red lanterns out front, and also more modern places with good sake lists and non-smoking sections. I've tried to include a few examples from each category in this chapter.

Other motsu dishes that you may run into are "motsu-yaki," which is grilled organ meats on skewers (often interchangeable with "yakiton") and "motsu-nabe," which is a more substantial hotpot stew that's prepared in large batches for two or more people.

Vocabulary

yakiton 焼きトン・やきとん	grilled skewers of pork and pork organ meats
motsu yaki もつ焼	grilled skewers of organ meats
harami ハラミ	tender pork diaphragm meat
bara ばら	rib meat
tan たん・タン	tongue
kashira かしら	pork cheeks
karubi カルビ	marinated short ribs
shiro しろ	intestines
tsukune つくね	grilled minced-meat patty
gyū motsu nikomi 牛もつ煮込み	beef organ-meat stew
buta motsu nikomi 豚もつ煮込み	pork organ-meat stew
tori motsu nikomi 鳥もつ煮込み	chicken giblet stew
motsu nabe もつ鍋	hotpot stew of beef or pork organ meats
horumon ホルモン	pork or beef organ meats, served raw or grilled

Teruteru (Takadanobaba)
やきとん てるてる

The first-rate grilled pork at Teruteru is matched by a serious selection of craft sake, with many seasonal choices. Yakiton skewers start at just ¥100, including more than a dozen different organ meats. The tsukune (minced-pork patty) is outstanding, a perfect balance of meaty flavors with a good amount of fat, and the shiro (intestines) and harami (tender diaphragm meat) are also highly recommended.

Balance your meal with excellent grilled zucchini, asparagus and other vegetables, or with the seasonal vegetable plate served bagna cauda style. The motsu nikomi is also quite hearty and satisfying, and goes very well with the more assertive sakes on the list. The setting is a very unpretentious izakaya-style pub, built around a long counter with a few small tables in back. Budget around ¥2000–2500 for food and drink.

Makotoya (Yotsuya 3-chome)
やきとん まことや

While grilled pork is the main draw at this charmingly casual neighborhood izakaya, they serve some excellent grilled chicken as well. Buta bara (pork belly on skewers) is one of the highlights, as is the bonjiri (fatty chicken tail). The sake seleciton is limited but they seem to always have at least one or two interesting seasonal labels, plus a good variety of shochu.

Prices are reasonable, and the old-school izakaya atmosphere is relaxed, although it can get a bit smoky at times depending on your neighbors. In addition to table seating there's also a large counter that's good for lone diners.

Buta Ichiro (Asakusabashi)
ぶたいちろう

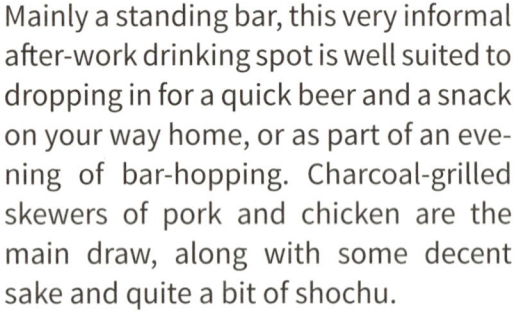

Mainly a standing bar, this very informal after-work drinking spot is well suited to dropping in for a quick beer and a snack on your way home, or as part of an evening of bar-hopping. Charcoal-grilled skewers of pork and chicken are the main draw, along with some decent sake and quite a bit of shochu.

Pork skewers start at just ¥100, and they're good value for the money, although a few of the meat items may be a bit more chewy than average. The karubi (rib meat) and harami (tender diaphragm meat) are favorites from the skewered-pork list, and the grilled scallops and chicken tsukune (minced chicken meatball) are also quite satisfying and nicely infused with charcoal flavors from grilling.

Pork motsu nikomi (¥290) is an excellent way to start things off while you're waiting for your meat to grill. The various organ meats are all distinctively flavored, interspersed with tasty chunks of daikon radish that have soaked up the rich broth. Overall the flavors are softer and gentler than a typical nikomi, and a good match for most drinks. The sake list is small, and focused on reliable labels like Kubota Senju (¥590 a glass).

There are standing areas both inside the shop and out front, with a bit of tatami seating upstairs. There's also a second branch with an identical menu right next door in case there's no room here. Budget around ¥2000 for food and drink.

Shimbashi Yakiton (Shimbashi)
新橋やきとん

As the shop name indicates, the specialty here is definitely yakiton—with some fourteen varieties of grilled pork starting at around ¥100. The Japanese menu has a neatly illustrated chart explaining where the various cuts of meat come from. Some favorites are the charcoal-infused tontoro (neck and shoulder meat) and harami (tender diaphragm meat), plus very nice tebasaki (chicken wings) from the smaller yakitori side of the menu.

For starters, big crisp chunks of cucumber in salt will help fill your vegetable quota for the day. The smooth, rich pork organ-meat stew (Motsu nikomi) is built on a miso base, but a subtle one—the overall flavor is more porky than miso-heavy. There are six different sake—three cold and three served at room temperature, although only the cold ones are listed on the English menu.

Patrons—mostly Shimbashi office workers stopping in for a drink on the way home—can stand at upturned barrels, communal tables or a long counter in front of the grill. The ceiling is festooned with paper lanterns advertising beer and liquor brands. There's also some outdoor standing space, which may be less smoky depending on your luck.

Budget around ¥1200–2500 for food and drink, depending on how long you stay. There are several other branches scattered throughout Tokyo, but this main branch has the best reputation for food.

Riki (Ikebukuro)
酒蔵 力 池袋西口店 （シュゾウ リキ）

Located just a minute or two from Ikebukuro station, this bustling izakaya is an easy stop for a quick bite and a drink on the way home, and the crowded ground-floor counter is full of solo diners as well as groups. Unlike most yakiton shops, they also have a take-out window in front where you can pick up skewers of grilled pork to go.

You'll be asked for your drink order as soon as you sit down; ask for oolong tea ('uroncha') if you don't feel like having a beer or a shochu cocktail. The grill menu (Japanese only) lists some eleven cuts of pork, five cuts of chicken, and four grilled vegetables, as well as plenty of side dishes. There's a chalkboard (also in Japanese only) with daily specials, including some fish and seafood.

The excellent pork karubi (short ribs) and kashira (pork cheeks) are both quite meaty, with subtle charcoal flavoring, while the liver is tender. The motsu nikomi here has a mild, almost creamy broth, letting the individual organ-meat flavors stand out. Note that there's a minimum order of two skewers for any particular grilled item.

Seating at the counter can be tight during busy times, but customers tend to come and go quickly. Budget around ¥2000–3000 for ample food and drink. This is the first Tokyo branch of a small Saitama-based izakaya chain.

Sasamoto (Ginza)
ささもと

Quite a bit more elegant than your typical yakiton specialist, Sasamoto has a tasteful retro-style decor, with tile floors, old movie and theater posters on the walls, and mid-century jazz on the stereo. The specialties of the house are grilled skewers of both pork and beef, with an emphasis on organ meats.

They're also known for their kushi-nikomi—pork giblets on skewers in a rich miso-based stew. You can order a la carte (there are around fifteen different grilled skewers), or take the easy approach with one of the set menus, starting at around ¥2000, that feature various grilled items plus one small portion of stew.

Some highlights here include both beef and pork skirt steaks, pork tongue grilled in miso, and tender pork liver. Braised cabbage served in a rich, fatty pork broth is also quite nice. Note that the shop doesn't provide chopsticks, so you're expected to eat directly from the skewer. Don't plan on sharing.

Numata (Shinjuku)
もつ煮込み専門店 沼田

Fans of beef motsu nikomi can choose three different varieties of stew at this stylish specialty izakaya. The soy sauce version best shows off the individual flavors of the various organ meats, while the miso and extra-spicy miso versions will satisfy those who like a richer, deeper sauce.

The tender braised beef tongue is also highly recommended, and it's definitely worth exploring the selection of charcoal-grilled beef, beef parts and vegetables. There are two or three premium sake, chosen to complement the rich nikomi and charcoal-infused flavors. Budget around ¥2500 for dinner with drinks.

Dandan (Kayabacho)
団だん

This very old-fashioned izakaya has a genuine shitamachi (traditional Tokyo) feel to it—sumo paraphernalia on the walls, colorful kites on the ceiling, a TV set going in the corner, and three big communal tables for customers. The shop is especially known for their beef motsu nikomi, a salty, intensely flavored miso-based stew featuring a variety of organ meats.

I'd recommend the tofu nikomi (¥350), which is the same stew but with several chunks of tofu to soak up the rich flavors. The rest of the menu tends towards snacks for drinking, such as roast duck. Bring your own napkins.

The drinks list includes seven or eight different sake, priced from ¥450 and served either room temperature or heated to one of three different levels; there are also one or two sake served cold.

Hikaru (Nakano)
燿（ヒカル）

Beef Motsu nikomi is one of the main menu items at this informal drinking spot, incorporating five different organ meats in a hearty, miso-heavy soup. The rest of the menu focuses on tasty drinking snacks like deep-fried chicken karaage and charcoal-grilled fish and vegetables, to go with the cheap cocktails and beer.

Budget around ¥3000 for food and drink, including ¥500 per person table charge.

Akatsuka (Akihabara)
赤津加

Surrounded by garish electronics shops and maid cafes, the curtained entrance to this old-school izakaya feels like a portal to another era. It's far from fancy inside, just an after-work drinking spot with a big wrap-around counter and ample table seating, with a TV set on in the background and cigarette smoke wafting from various tables.

The kitchen turns out a typical selection of sashimi, grilled meats and fish, but many people come here specifically for their tori motsu nikomi (chicken giblet stew). It's served steaming hot, with a richly flavored miso-based broth balanced by silky tofu, big sweet chunks of onion and pungent scallions.

The sake selection is also very old-school, so you might want to stick to beer or shochu cocktails. A hefty serving of stew with a small beer will run ¥1600, or budget around ¥3000 for dinner with drinks.

More motsu nikomi

- **Jidoriya** (ぢどり屋) in Nakano, just a few minutes away from Hikaru (above), does an excellent Kyushu-style version of beef motsu nikomi. See the chapter on "Regional Dishes" (page 79) for details.

Data

Teruteru (Takadanobaba)   03-6908-8351
やきとん てるてる
Takadanobaba 3-22-4, Shinjuku-ku
Open 5pm-midnight (Sun -11pm) daily.

Makotoya (Yotsuya 3-chome)   03-6380-0829
やきとん まことや
Arakicho 1-1, Shinjuku-ku
Open 5pm-midnight. Closed Sundays.

Buta Ichiro (Asakusabashi)   03-3863-9550
ぶたいちろう
Asakusabashi 1-9-9, Taito-ku
Open 5pm-midnight (LO) daily.

Shimbashi Yakiton (Shimbashi)   03-3539-4838
新橋やきとん
Shimbashi 1-14-8, Minato-ku
Open 4-11pm (LO). Closed Sundays.

Riki (Ikebukuro)   03-5957-5529
酒蔵 力 池袋西口店 （シュゾウ リキ）
Nishi-Ikebukuro 1-15-3, Toshima-ku
Open 3-10:30pm (LO) daily.

Sasamoto (Ginza)   03-3564-5881
ささもと
Hanabishi Bldg 1F, Ginza 4-3-7, Chuo-ku
Open 4:30-11pm. Closed Mondays.

Numata (Shinjuku)   03-3350-5029
もつ煮込み専門店 沼田
Shinjuku 3-6-3, 2F, Shinjuku-ku
Open 5pm-midnight daily.

Dandan (Kayabacho)   03-3551-4920
団だん
Shinkawa 1-8-20, Chuo-ku
Open 5-10pm. Closed weekends.

Hikaru (Nakano) — 03-3388-8778
燿
Nakano 5-47-3, Nakano-ku
Open 5pm-1am daily.

Akatsuka (Akihabara) — 03-3251-2585
赤津加
Soto-Kanda 1-10-2, Chiyoda-ku
Open 11:30am-1:30, 5-10:30pm. Closed weekends.

Yakitori

(grilled chicken)

焼き鳥

Yakitori, grilled chicken on skewers, is a good example of the charms of B-kyu cuisine—it's a very straightforward and uncomplicated food, but when it's done just right the results are sublimely delicious. Individual shops take pride in the quality of the chicken and other ingredients they use, their home-made basting sauces, and in particular their grilling skills.

You can get skewers of chicken to take home from department-store food halls, supermarkets or even convenience stores, but the best yakitori is served at izakaya-style pubs, grilled to order, preferably over good-quality charcoal. Because of the time-consuming nature of the grilling process, it's not well suited to hectic Tokyo lunch hours, so you'll usually find it only in the evening; when yakitori shops are open at lunchtime they usually offer a limited menu of rice-based dishes.

How to order

When you order, you can specify the cuts of the bird that you want, and whether you prefer your skewer grilled with salt (shio) or with sauce (tare). I usually ask for salt, as it allows the quality of the chicken to shine through, but you can ask which they recommend (osusume?), or alternate for different skewers. There's usually a platter of assorted cuts (moriawase) available, but these often focus on organ meats that you may or may not like; I prefer ordering individual skewers.

Chicken wings are a good way to judge the quality of a shop—ideally they're grilled for a relatively long time, resulting in a crisp, lightly charred skin with still-succulent meat. Sometimes the cook will rush the process if they're in a hurry, though, with less than ideal results. Bonjiri (chicken tail meat) is another interesting cut when it's available—

it's extremely fatty and juicy, so ideally the skin should be adequately grilled to balance out the fat.

Seseri, chicken neck, is not always on offer, but when you can find it it's worth a try for its nice balance of meat and fat. Tsukune, chicken meatballs, vary quite a bit from shop to shop, but they're usually very tasty, often incorporating bits of cartilage for a crunchy texture. And don't forget your vegetables—yakitori shops do nicely grilled mushrooms, green peppers and bacon-wrapped asparagus, as well as crunchy raw cucumbers with miso and other vegetable side dishes.

Jars of powdered shichimi red pepper are provided on the counter or table, and you can sprinkle some onto your chicken to spice it up. There will also be some sort of receptacle where you can deposit your used skewers.

Premium birds

Foreign visitors are sometimes surprised when they run across chicken sashimi on the menu of an upscale yakitori shop. They may wonder—Is this chicken really served raw? The answer is yes—it's raw or maybe lightly seared, served sashimi style with soy sauce and perhaps some wasabi for seasoning. Chicken that's served this way will be from small farms where they raise very healthy chickens in a sterile environment that's been set up for this purpose—the very opposite of a factory farm. While there are no guarantees in life, it may be reassuring to learn that many people in Japan eat raw chicken on a regular basis, and if a restaurant serves raw chicken it means that it's been hygienically raised.

Gourmet yakitori shops often advertise that they use "jidori" chickens from particular regions of Japan. Generally raised as free-range birds, these are either heirloom native breeds of chicken or hybrids where at least half the DNA comes from native breeds. Some famous regional birds prized for their superior flavor are Cochin from Nagoya, Satsuma-dori from Kyushu, and Hinai-dori from Akita. Depending on the season, you might also run into other birds like duck, guinea fowl and quail on the menu.

Yakitori shops to explore

While yakitori can reach high levels of culinary achievement, and high prices to match, sometimes you just want a few nice skewers and a cold beer in a noisy after-work pub. In choosing the shops in this section, I've picked some places that have a lively atmosphere and a fun, budget-friendly experience, while others are more focused on top-quality ingredients and a refined atmosphere. I've also included one place (Isehiro) that serves freshly grilled chicken at lunchtime. There are hundreds more yakitori shops to explore, but hopefully this will be a good start.

Vocabulary

yakitori やきとり・焼鳥　grilled chicken

shio 塩　(grilled with) salt

tare タレ　(grilled with) sauce

momo もも　chicken thigh meat

negima ねぎま・ネギ間　chicken pieces and leek

sasami 笹身・ささみ　chicken breast meat

teba 手羽　chicken wing

tebasaki 手羽先　chicken wing or wing tip

tsukune つくね　minced chicken patty

kawa かわ・皮　chicken skin

bonjiri ぼんじり　fatty chicken tail

seseri せせり　chicken neck meat

rebā レバー　liver

sunagimo 砂肝　gizzard

sunazuri 砂ずり・砂ズリ　gizzard

hatsu はつ・ハツ　heart

shōniku 正肉　boneless meat with skin

uzura うずら　quail (egg)

negi ねぎ・葱　leek

shishitō ししとう・獅子唐　small Japanese green pepper

ginnan 銀杏・ぎんなん　ginkgo nut

shiitake 椎茸・しいたけ　shiitake mushroom

piiman ピーマン　green pepper (often stuffed)

jidori 地鶏　heritage-breed chicken or hybrid

torisashi 鳥刺し　raw chicken

Nagoya kōchin 名古屋コーチン　Cochin, an heirloom breed chicken

shamo 軍鶏・しゃも　a game bird with slightly chewy meat

kamo 鴨　wild duck

aigamo 合鴨　a cross between wild duck and domesticated duck

suzume すずめ　sparrow (or young chicken)

horohorochō ホロホロ鳥　guinea fowl

Hachibei (Roppongi)
焼とりの八兵衛 六本木店

While excellent yakitori is the centerpiece of the menu at this stylish basement izakaya, there's much more in store—beautiful charcoal-grilled seasonal vegetables, creative side dishes, and a surprisingly big wine list. Hachibei's main branch is in Hakata (aka Fukuoka in northern Kyushu), so there's a nice selection of Kyushu regional fare as well.

The chicken here is artfully grilled over the finest charcoal, and the results are tender, moist and very flavorful. The sasami umeshiso (chicken breast fillets with plum and shiso) is particularly good, and chicken wings have pleasingly crunchy skin without being dry. As is the style in Fukuoka, the grilled chicken is served with vinegared cabbage, which serves as a refreshing, high-fiber palate cleanser between skewers.

Some non-chicken highlights here are the rather fatty grilled pork belly, grilled bamboo shoots (in season) served with a spicy miso paste, and deep-fried edamame green-pea fritters on skewers. The Caesar salad, topped with very nice home-cured bacon, is also worth a try.

The drinks menu features more than two dozen wines (¥3400–12,800 per bottle), plus six kinds of shochu, two umeshu, and four well-chosen sakes from Kyushu. Budget around ¥6000 for food and drink.

Doromamire (Yotsuya 3-chome)
どろまみれ

The chicken here, heirloom-breed Hinai-dori birds from Akita, is good enough to eat raw, and indeed the shop's chicken sashimi dishes are among my favorites, as are their chicken liver skewers, which are served quite rare. Other standouts are the seseri (neck meat), which delivers lots of delicious grilled fat while being satisfyingly meaty, and the sasami (breast meat), pleasantly charcoally with a sharp dollop of ume (plum) or wasabi to really bring out its flavor. And don't miss the big, oblong-shaped tsukune meatballs—juicy and lightly crunchy—with an optional raw egg for dipping.

Doromamire takes equal pride in its seasonal vegetables, and there are around twenty vegetables featured on the menu, served grilled, in salads, and in creative arrangements like the summertime corn tempura or the avocado sashimi. Cream cheese marinated in miso paste makes an interesting amuse-bouche between courses. Sake fans can choose from a dozen craft sake, including multiple labels from the same brewery. Budget around ¥4000–5000 at dinnertime for food and drink.

Sōten (Minami-guchi, Ōtsuka)
蒼天 南口店

Sōten stands out from the crowd thanks to the high quality of their birds, the creativity of their side dishes and their excellent selection of craft sake. Ordering one of the seasonal set menus is a good strategy here—they change every month, and feature game birds when available. During one mid-autumn visit I enjoyed a delicious confit of tiny quail legs, tender guinea fowl, and skewers of fatty wild duck over the course of the evening.

Richly flavored appetizers like blue cheese and chicken-liver pate with raisin bread and smoked chicken will start a meal off in high gear. From the regular, year-round menu, recommendations include the moist and beautifully seasoned tsukune (chicken meatballs), which are crunchier than average thanks to an ample helping of ground cartilage in the recipe. Chicken wings are grilled perfectly, passing the crispness test without a hint of dryness.

Almost everything here is served shio-style (salted) rather than with sauce, but one exception is the liver—it's prepared semi-raw, and is extremely tender, with a sweetish sauce that complements the flavor. (There's also raw chicken sashimi on the menu.) Chicken courses are broken up by some nice side dishes, such as a very original chawan mushi that incorporates mozzarella and tiny tomatoes alongside the more traditional chicken, shiitake mushrooms and gingko nuts, to suprisingly good effect.

The sake selection includes several varieties of Sōten's own custom-label Kozaemon sake from Gifu, plus another two dozen well-selected brands from small breweries around the country. Budget around ¥6000–7000 for dinner with drinks, and bring cash; they don't take credit cards.

Isehiro (Kyōbashi)
伊勢廣

Unlike most yakitoriya in town, Isehiro fires up the charcoal at lunchtime in order to serve full sets of freshly grilled skewers rather than just quick rice-based dishes. And lunch is outstanding—starting with premium heirloom-breed chickens, the chefs grill every cut to perfection. Gizzards and sasami are tender and moist, with a bit of wasabi kick to the sasami, while the tsukune is juicy and pleasantly crunchy in texture.

The lunch set comes with a nice chicken skin broth to start things off, and first-rate pickles to accompany your rice. The setting is rather old-fashioned, with fairly tight seating at the counter and communal table, and tatami seating upstairs. Lunchtime menus are priced ¥1550–3850, or budget around ¥8000 at dinnertime.

Akita Pure Rice Sake Bar (Yaesu)
秋田純米酒処

If you love good craft sake and you love good chicken, you really should know about this rather unique bar. It is located in front of a yakitori shop called Abeya Honke, and if you sit at the bar you can sample tasting flights of Akita sake—three, five or seven small glasses at a time—while you enjoy skewers of first-rate chicken from the restaurant.

The chicken is premium Hinai-dori birds from Akita, and while the menu offers excellent versions of all the usual skewers, if you're feeling adventurous the sashimi assortment, with five different cuts of raw chicken, is a revelation. The sake selection offers more than three dozen varieties on any given day, focusing on small breweries in Akita Prefecture and featuring limited-edition seasonal specials and prototype bottles.

Sake is mostly priced from ¥580–880 per glass, while a seven-glass tasting flight is ¥1600. Budget around ¥2000–3000 for some skewers and drinks. The shop is located in the second-floor Kitamachi Dining complex at the north end of the Yaesu side of Tokyo Station, above the Kitchen Street and Kurobei Yokocho dining complexes.

ZenyaRen (Ōtemachi)
全や連 総本店

It's Japan's first yakitori theme park! Seven famous yakitori shops from around the country have gathered in one spot, allowing Tokyo diners to compare their skewers side by side. The styles and flavors represented here are surprisingly diverse, and the setting is lively and fun—a massive 200-seat space divided up into cozy dining niches for groups of various sizes.

ZenyaRen's menu is also massive: Each participating shop offers their own array of individual skewers (some with pork as well as chicken), side dishes and combination platters. Some skewers are better than others—this is the type of menu that rewards exploration over multiple visits—but the fifteen-skewer mixed assortment (¥1980) with representative items from each shop might be one place to start. Some recommended side dishes include the Kyoto-style pickles on skewers and the steamed vegetables with sesame-based dipping sauce.

Several decent regional sake are available to accompany your skewers, along with many other drink options, and you can choose from the budget-friendly open-bar plans if you're making a night of it. While there may be better yakitori in town, ZenyaRen offers an appealing combination of a fun setting, reasonable prices and a huge selection.

Hakata Mangetsu (Ebisu)
博多満月 恵比寿店

Sometimes you're in the mood for cheap and very casual yakitori, and this lively basement izakaya fills the bill. They attract a relatively young, diverse crowd and have a charming style all their own: mismatched sofas and chairs that look like they've put in years of service, an infectiously bouncy eighties-pop soundtrack, and laid-back but friendly service. Plus prices that are hard to believe in such a prime location—yakitori from ¥46 per skewer and beer from ¥199 per glass.

The food is fairly decent and good value for the money, with some nice bargain surprises like the very good cabbage with spicy miso dip (¥300). In addition to yakitori there's a selection of filling nabe stews, starting at ¥924 per person, along with other izakaya standards. The grilled pork is a favorite here, and the chicken breast with wasabi is consistently good.

Drinks include fruit liqueurs, Korean makkoli, sake, shochu, wine and cocktails. Budget around ¥2000–2500 for ample food and drink.

More yakitori

- Several of the shops listed in the section covering yakiton (grilled pork) also serve grilled chicken; most of them are at the very casual and inexpensive end of the spectrum.

Data

Hachibei (Roppongi) — 03-3475-1689
焼とりの八兵衛 六本木店
Roppongi 7-4-5, B1F, Minato-ku
Open 6pm-12:30am (LO). Closed Sundays.

Doromamire (Yotsuya 3-chome) — 03-6380-1197
どろまみれ
Yakata Bldg 2F, Arakicho 20, Shinjuku-ku
Open 6pm-1am (LO; Sat -10pm). Closed Sundays.

Sōten (Minami-guchi, Ōtsuka) — 03-5944-8105
蒼天 南口店
Minami-Otsuka 3-39-13, Toshima-ku
Open 5:30-11pm. Closed Mondays.

Isehiro (Kyōbashi) — 03-3281-5864
伊勢廣
Kyobashi 1-5-4, Chuo-ku
Open 11:30am-2, 4:30-9pm. Closed Sundays.

Akita Pure Rice Sake Bar (Yaesu) — 03-6269-9277
秋田純米酒処
Kitamachi Dining (2F), Marunouchi 1-9-1, Chiyoda-ku
Open 11am-10pm (LO; Sat, Sun -9pm) daily.

ZenyaRen (Ōtemachi) — 03-3231-7705
全や連 総本店
Tokyo Sankei Bldg B2F, Otemachi 1-7-2, Chiyoda-ku
Open 5-10pm (LO; Sat, Sun from 11am) daily.

Hakata Mangetsu (Ebisu) 03-6408-9460
博多満月 恵比寿店
Daikoku Bldg B1F, Ebisu 1-8-14, Shibuya-ku
Open 5pm-5am daily.

Beef tongue and more meat dishes
牛タン、他の肉料理

Beef tongue ('gyūtan' in Japanese) is a regional specialty of the Sendai area in Miyagi Prefecture, about ninety minutes north of Tokyo by train. Thick-cut, charcoal-grilled tongue is the main attraction at tongue restaurants, and at its best it has a tender but meaty texture, not too chewy, with a hint of charcoal flavor. It can be flavored with just salt and pepper, or marinated in miso. It's served with wasabi and very spicy pickles, often as part of a set meal with soup and barley-flavored rice.

Most restaurants also offer dishes like tongue stew, tongue curry and tongue sausages. Braised tongue (yude-tan) is a bit less common, but it's worth a try if it's on the menu, with very tender meat seasoned with black pepper and served in a rich broth with a bit of wasabi to bring out the flavor.

Miyagi Prefecture is a famous sake-producing region, so

you can often find local craft sakes on the drinks list, along with red wine and the usual beer and soft drinks.

Horse meat is another regional dish that you'll occasionally run into in Tokyo. It's served grilled, in stews, or raw as horse-meat sashimi (basashi), and it's popular locally in several parts of Japan such as Kumamoto Prefecture (in Kyushu), Nagano Prefecture and Yamanashi Prefecture. In Tokyo it's most often served in izakaya-style pubs that specialize in regional cuisines.

Vocabulary

gyūtan 牛タン beef tongue

gyūtan-yaki 牛たん焼 grilled beef tongue

sumibi-yaki 炭火焼き charcoal-grilled

aburiyaki 炙り焼き charcoal-grilled

yude-tan ゆでたん boiled, braised tongue

tsukune つくね grilled minced meat

shichū シチュー stew

karē カレー curry

sōsēji ソーセージ sausage

tēru sūpu テールスープ oxtail soup

teishoku 定食 set meal

ichi-nin mae 1人前 portion for one person

ichi-ten-go-nin mae 1.5人前 1.5 x portion for one person

baniku 馬肉 horse meat

basashi 馬刺し raw horse meat (sashimi)

shikaniku 鹿肉 venison

gyūniku 牛肉 beef

Beef tongue

Shinobu (Yotsuya)
たん焼 忍

This unpretentious Yotsuya izakaya serves some of the best beef tongue in Tokyo. Shinobu's braised tongue (yude-tan) in particular is the pride of the kitchen and the shop's best seller—incredibly tender and richly flavored, and perfectly complemented by a small dab of wasabi. The tender charcoal-grilled tongue is another standout—served with excellent pickled hakusai, it somehow packs in more flavor per bite than grilled tongue at other shops.

Tongue stew and a few more tongue variations round out the small menu, along with some nice vegetable dishes like stewed daikon and broccoli ohitashi. Sake is limited to one cold and one hot variety, so beer might be a better choice. The atmosphere is lively and service is friendly, although seating, especially in the non-smoking counter area, is rather rudimentary.

Budget around ¥5000–6000 for a full meal with drinks, or less if you're just stopping in for a snack. The shop is very popular—there's almost always a line outside—so call ahead to reserve your spot.

Vector Beer (Shinjuku Gyoen-mae)
ベクタービア

It may look like just another Tokyo craft-beer bar, but Vector serves up an appealing menu of beef-tongue dishes and other solid izakaya fare, making it a popular dining destination as well as a bar. The charcoal-grilled sumibi-yaki tongue (¥980) is a crowd favorite—slightly chewy and cut a bit thinner than average, with a nice charcoal-infused flavor that's complemented by the accompanying wasabi and crunchy pickled hakusai.

There's plenty more tongue in store—tongue and mushroom ajillo, two kinds of tongue meatballs, tongue demi-glace stew, home-made tongue ham, tongue cutlet and menchi-katsu (deep-fried minced tongue). The tongue rillettes (¥480) are a good quick-starter dish while you're waiting for your grilled and fried items.

Vector is also one of the better craft beer bars in town, with ten taps dispensing a well-chosen selection from Japanese and US small breweries, all at very reasonable prices. Three-beer tasting sets (¥1000) are a great way to compare different breweries and styles, and the bar's convenient late-night hours are another bonus. Budget around ¥3500 for dinner and drinks.

Date no Gyūtan (Marunouchi)
伊達の牛たん 本舗

The charcoal-grilled beef tongue at this Sendai-based shop comes in a choice of miso or salt-grilled, or you can get a combination of the two—I recommend the salt as it brings out the charcoal flavoring better. The tongue itself is pleasantly chewy, and comes in thick-cut and extra-thick-cut versions, in regular and extra-large portions, all with excellent pickles on the side. The minced-tongue tsukune is another highlight here, although the spicy dip that it comes with is a bit superfluous.

Other specialty dishes are a tongue nikomi stew and a classic European-style tongue stew with a rich demi-glace sauce, both of them showcasing very tender braised meat. Drinks options include seven kinds of Miyagi Prefecture sake and New World and European wines. Budget around ¥2000–3000 at dinnertime.

Rikyū (Ikebukuro)
牛たん炭焼 利久

One of several Tokyo outlets of this popular Sendai-based beef-tongue specialist, this branch offers an especially wide menu. The more than a dozen dishes range from tongue sausages, meatballs, and deep-fried tongue to curries, European-style stews and tongue sushi. The piece de resistance though is the excellent charcoal-grilled tongue. The menu is rounded out by creative and original izakaya fare, with a nice selection of Sendai-area sake to wash it all down.

Conveniently located in a shopping complex inside Ikebukuro station, Rikyu stays open all afternoon for late lunchgoers and snack-seekers. Several teishoku-style set menus cater to diners who just want a quick meal, and in particular the "Marutoku Rikyu Set" (¥1674) is a satisfying and budget-friendly introduction to the shop's offerings. It includes a half-order each of grilled tongue and a choice of tongue curry or stew, plus oxtail soup, smoked-tongue salad and rice.

The tongue curry is quite tasty—it's a spicy Euro-Japanese version, with a roux made by blending Indian spices in a French-style stew base. (Other options are the more Indian-influenced keema curry or a milder tongue stew.) The oxtail soup is pleasantly beefy in flavor, with substantial chunks of meat and lots of leeks, and some demonstratively spicy miso-marinated pickles liven up the grilled-tongue platter.

If you're not in a hurry and want to explore the full menu, numerous small dishes are waiting to be sampled. Smoked tongue—part of an hors d'oeuvre plate—is beautifully spiced, and the beef-tongue tsukune (grilled meatball on a stick) is much meatier than the usual chicken version. Another favorite is the tongue kakuni stew, with tender, slow-cooked meat that's full of vibrant flavors.

The drinks list includes half a dozen local sake brands from Miyagi Prefecture, including Rikyu's own house brand of sake. I can recommend their daiginjo, or the three-glass tasting set if you want some variety. Budget around ¥3000–4500 for a full meal with drinks, or ¥1200–1600 for a quick teishoku set. There's a solid selection of take-away tongue too—from vacuum-packed charcoal-grilled tongue to pre-cooked pouches of stews and curries. (Other Tokyo branches are in Akasaka, Kichijoji, Tokyo Station and elsewhere around town.)

More meat dishes

Gyūhachi (Kōenji)
牛八 高円寺店

Located under the JR railroad tracks, this very casual drinking spot serves great charcoal-grilled beef on skewers, including a variety of organ meats. Surrounded by similarly inexpensive and informal shops, it makes a nice stop on a bar-hopping tour of the neighborhood. Budget around ¥2000 for food and drink.

HaruKor (Ōkubo)
ハルコロ

Ezo venison from Hokkaido is featured in several different dishes here at Tokyo's only Ainu restaurant, including a tasty venison steak and even better grilled venison with tangy ponzu sauce. Similar to Hokkaido country-style cooking, Ainu cuisine uses a bit more garlic, ginger and spices while focusing on seasonal local vegetables and other ingredients.

Besides venison, HaruKor also serves fresh Hokkaido salmon, scallops, potatoes and mountain vegetables, prepared in simple fashion to bring out their wholesome, natural flavors. Some standouts are the pan-fried scallops, asparagus and bacon; garlic fried rice with scallops and mustard greens; and gyoza dumplings. The dumplings are stuffed with kitopiro, a wild garlic-like grass similar to nira and only one of the several mysterious food names on the menu that I had to ask about.

Drinks include a few different Hokkaido sakes as well as shochu and beer. Like many of its neighboring Okubo shops, HaruKor features extremely casual decor and cheap prices—budget around ¥2000–2500 for food and drink.

Bakuro Kanda South (Kanda)
闇焼 馬喰ろう 神田南口店

Bakuro is set up like a yakiniku barbecue restaurant, with a small grill and exhaust chimney at each table, so you can grill your chosen cuts of horse meat and vegetables at your own pace. The big "oba" steak is quite good—a thick cut of meat with a good amount of fat, seasoned simply with salt and pepper. Our waiter prepared this for us at the table, cutting the meat into bite-size chunks with a pair of scissors. Kimchee and namuru are available as side dishes, just like in a regular yakiniku spot.

Don't neglect Bakuro's other specialty though—raw horse meat. The assorted sashimi platter featuring five different cuts of meat is most highly recommended (¥1080 for two)—all the cuts are very tender, and this is a great way to compare the different flavors. Yukke, minced raw horsemeat mixed with raw egg, onions and soy sauce, is sweeter and less spicy than your typical Korean beef yukke, and also worth a try.

Shochu is the main drink here, but they usually have a few seasonal craft sake available upon request, as well as Korean makkoli. The dining room is attractively appointed, with sufficient space around tables to keep it from feeling crowded. There's no counter, though; the place is set up mainly for pairs or groups of diners. Budget around ¥3000 for dinner with drinks.

Nikuzushi (Iidabashi)
肉寿司 神楽坂 みちくさ横丁

If you don't mind the informal setting, this unpretentious back-alley izakaya is a great place to explore the mysterious delights of horse-meat sushi and other raw-meat delicacies. The ten-piece Kagurazaka sushi platter (¥3200) is a good starting point—it includes a few different cuts of horse along with lightly seared chicken and raw wagyu beef, all prepared as sushi.

If you want to add on individual pieces, the a la carte menu offers beef, chicken and lamb options as well as several cuts of horse, and the rich "foie gras" sushi can be recommended whole-heartedly. To balance your diet and complement the meaty fare, there's an interesting selection of fresh vegetable dishes—ripe avocado sashimi (with pungent wasabi), raw turnip chunks and crisp cucumbers served with miso paste.

Drinks are reasonably priced and include a few premium sake brands as well as beer and shochu. Nikuzushi is located in the middle of an ancient-looking alleyway full of tiny drinking spots. There are around six counter seats on the ground floor and three small tables upstairs, reached via a steep and narrow stairway. Although it may seem like a casual, walk-in kind of spot, reservations are highly recommended if you're visiting at dinnertime.

Data

Shinobu (Yotsuya) — 03-3355-6338
たん焼き 忍
Saneicho 16, Shinjuku-ku
Open 5-10:30pm (LO). Closed Sundays.

Vector Beer (Shinjuku Gyoen-mae) — 03-6380-0742
ベクタービア
Hotel Park Inn 1F, Shinjuku 1-36-5, Shinjuku-ku
Open 5pm-1am (LO, Sat -11:30). Closed Sundays.

Date no Gyūtan (Marunouchi) — 03-6256-0810
伊達の牛たん 本舗
JP Tower Kitte B1F, Marunouchi 2-7-2, Chiyoda-ku
Open 10am-9pm (LO; Sun -8pm) daily.

Rikyū (Ikebukuro) — 03-5952-0404
牛たん炭焼 利久
Esola Ikebukuro 7F, Nishi-Ikebukuro 1-12-1, Toshima-ku
Open 11am-10pm (LO) daily.

Gyūhachi (Kōenji) — 03-3310-0555
牛八 高円寺店
Koenji-Minami 3-69-1, Suginami-ku
Open 4pm-midnight daily.

HaruKor (Ōkubo) — 03-3368-4677
ハルコロ
Hyakunincho 1-10-1, Shinjuku-ku
Open 5pm-midnight daily.

Bakuro Kanda South (Kanda) — 03-3516-8348
闇焼 馬喰ろう 神田南口店
Nihonbashi Hongokucho 4-4-12, Chuo-ku
Open 5-11:29pm (Sat 4-10). Closed Sundays.

Nikuzushi (Iidabashi) — 050-5786-8216
肉寿司 神楽坂 みちくさ横丁
Michikusa Yokocho, Kagurazaka 1-14, Shinjuku-ku
Open 5pm-5am (Sun 4-12) daily.

Kushiage

(deep-fried skewers)

串揚げ

Kushiage is a style of cooking where individual morsels of food (seafood, meats, vegetables) are placed on skewers, then dipped in batter and breading before being dunked in a deep-fryer. Depending on the restaurant, finished skewers may be served with salt, lemon, dipping sauces and other condiments, and basic ingredients may be stuffed with cheese or wrapped in bacon or shiso leaves. It's often hard to tell exactly what's inside a finished skewer, so some of the fun of kushiage is the surprise of discovering just what you're eating.

A regional cuisine of the Osaka area, kushiage has developed a following in Tokyo as well. Specialty restaurants come in a wide range of styles, from elegant dining rooms with high prices to casual izakaya-style setups. Some of the fancier places use an "omakase" system where they serve you skewer after skewer of their recommendations of the day until you tell them to stop. Moriawase (assortment) menus are also common, where you can choose an assortment of eight or ten or twelve preselected skewers, usually at a price that's cheaper than ordering a la carte.

Note that some of the pricier kushiage restaurants offer much less expensive lunch specials.

Vocabulary

kushiage	串揚げ	deep-fried meat, seafood and vegetables on skewers
omakase	お任せ・おまかせ	chef's assortment
moriawase	盛り合わせ	assortment
buta(niku)	豚(肉)	pork
chikin	チキン	chicken
tori	鳥・とり	chicken
gyū(niku)	牛(肉)	beef
ebi	えび・海老	prawn, shrimp
ika	いか	squid
kisu	キス	whiting (fish)
hotate	帆立・ホタテ	scallops
nasu	茄子・なす	eggplant, aubergine
renkon	れんこん・蓮根	lotus root
shiitake	椎茸・しいたけ	shiitake mushroom
asupara	アスパラ	asparagus
tamanegi	たまねぎ・玉葱	onion
kabocha	かぼちゃ・南瓜	pumpkin
(puchi) tomato	(プチ)トマト	(baby) tomato
kamanbēru	カマンベール	Camembert cheese
chiizu	チーズ	(with) cheese
bēkon maki	ベーコン巻	wrapped in bacon

Teppen (Otemachi)
なかめのてっぺん 丸の内

This lively after-work izakaya serves up great kushiage. Delicate in flavor, with a thin breading and very little oiliness, the skewers don't even need sauce, just a bit of salt to enhance the natural flavors. An assortment platter of six skewers runs ¥1100, or you can choose from ten different varieties by the piece (or try them all). The anago (eel) is a standout, as is the very fresh-tasting asparagus and the reasonably hefty chunk of foie gras.

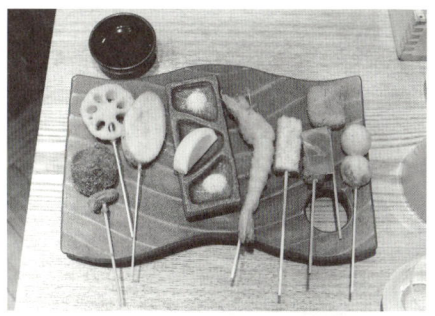

The otoshi here (the starter that comes with your table charge) is a box of fresh, crisp vegetables with a salty, buttery bagna-cauda-style hot dip. While kushiage is the most popular item on the menu, you'll also find an excellent selection of charcoal-grilled fish and seafood, premium meats and seasonal vegetables. Some recommendations include the grilled beef tongue, smoked bacon, grilled asparagus and eggplant. The premium sake and shochu lists are also worth checking out. Budget around ¥4000 for ample food and drink.

[While this is mainly a group destination, there is a counter area in case you're dining alone.]

Rokuhara (Akasaka)
六波羅

Top-quality seafood, meats and vegetables go into the kushiage here, and while the average dinnertime budget is around ¥6000, lunch is a real bargain at just ¥1000. The set lunch features eight assorted deep-fried skewers, and since it's the only thing on the menu you can just take a seat at the counter and wait for your freshly fried skewers to arrive, one by one, on your plate.

A recent seasonal selection included more deluxe ingredients than expected for the price—tasty whitefish and baby scallops and remarkably tender squid. Even the multi-colored diced pickles are fancier than average. Lunchtime service is friendly and quite efficient, although seating can be a bit tight if it's crowded. No lunch on weekends.

Tanaka (Shinjuku)
串カツ田中 新宿3丁目店

This popular Osaka-based izakaya is the complete opposite of your typical gourmet kushiage shop—the atmosphere is lively and often raucous, with every inch of the tightly packed tables crowded to overflowing with trays of food and drinks. And, true to their Osaka roots, prices are cheap—most deep-fried skewers are ¥100–120 each, with luxury items like asparagus and scallops just ¥200.

There are assortment platters if you want to start with the

basics (pork and beef cutlets and various vegetables), or you can jump right in with the more unusual items among the menu's forty choices—deep-fried ginger root, garlic cloves, pickles, liver, shishamo. Fried bananas are always a nice idea, and the ones here make a great dessert course alongside deep-fried mangos and "cookies and cream"—two battered and fried Oreo-like cookies.

Drinks are also quite inexpensive, which helps to explain the impressive noise level of the room—whiskey-based cocktails start at ¥350, and Tanaka has their own label of rough but serviceable one-cup sake, also ¥350. One important thing to note is the shop's sauce policy—double-dipping is strictly prohibited. You can dip each skewer into the communal sauce container only once, before you take a bite. If you want a bit more sauce after that, you can use a pristine raw cabbage leaf as a dipping utensil to transfer more sauce to your plate.

(Open from 2 pm weekends; LO 12:30 am Sundays and holidays.) [No counter seating; this is primarily a group dining destination.]

Kushinobo Bekkan (Shinjuku)
串の坊 新宿伊勢丹会館店

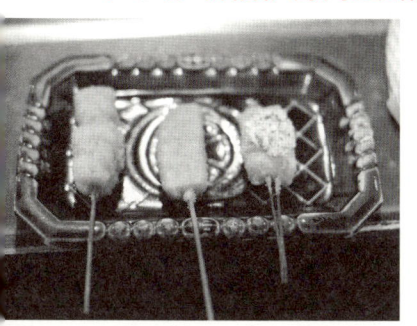

One of Tokyo's most reliable kushiage shops, Kushinobo offers creative skewers, a decent sake selection and good value for money. A ten-skewer set menu is ¥3240 at dinnertime, just one of many set-menu and a la carte options. The eight-skewer lunch set with soup and rice (¥1080) is a nice introduction—a recent seasonal selection featured salmon, green pepper stuffed with ground pork, prawn, chicken with celery and other delicacies, all served fresh and piping hot from the fryer.

This particular branch has all non-smoking seats; there's another branch upstairs on the eighth floor in the same building for smokers.

[Seating is all at the counter, making it comfortable for solo diners.]

Soba Kichi (Marunouchi)
ソバキチ

This popular after-work drinking spot offers very affordable prices—you can enjoy a couple of drinks and snacks here for under ¥2000. Deep-fried kushiage skewers start at around ¥140, and you can supplement your skewers with grilled pork belly, chicken cutlet or soba noodles.

The kushiage is rustic in style, with a thick, rough layer of batter that's fried to a satisfyingly crunchy consistency. Some recommendations include skewers of curry-flavored pork belly (buta bara), deep-fried cheese, chicken breast with ume (plum), shrimp and scallops. The latter two are ¥250 per skewer, the most expensive items on the menu.

One big drawing card here is the stylish setting, with warm lighting and a sleek central blond-wood counter contrasting with the coolly lit terrace garden and the Marunouchi night sky just beyond the windows. The atmosphere tends to be quite lively, and there's often a crowd here until midnight and beyond, unusual for this business-district neighborhood.

The restaurant is part of the Shin-Maru Building's seventh-floor "House" complex, and it's open until 4 am every night but Sunday. Limited English menus are available.

[This is mainly a group dining venue, although solo diners can sit at the counter.]

Kushiya Monogatari (Nishi-Shinjuku)
串家物語 新宿西口大ガード店

Ninety minutes of do-it-yourself deep-fried fun can be yours for just ¥2500 at this conveniently located branch of a popular Osaka-based chain. Help yourself to skewers of tasty chicken and pork, salmon and prawns, lotus root and broccoli from the refrigerated display cases, then batter them up yourself and plunge them into hot oil right at your table. There are always a few dozen items to choose from, the selection changing with the season.

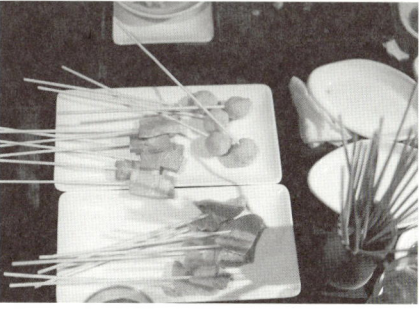

Seven different dipping sauces are available to liven up your finished skewers, and you can supplement your skewers with a do-it-yourself salad, soup, side dishes like curry rice and a few dessert items. There's even a chocolate fountain. Besides the all-you-can-eat deals, there are also open-bar plans offering beer and cocktails. Bring cash, though; they don't take credit cards. Lunch is served on weekends only, and reservations are strongly suggested.

[No counter seating; the restaurant is set up for group dining.]

More kushiage

- **Ippoippo** (一歩一歩), listed in the gyukatsu chapter (page 99), offers a nice selection of kushiage skewers at dinnertime, along with beef cutlet, sashimi and good craft sake in a casual izakaya setting.
- **Yabaton Kitte Granche** (矢場とん 東京KITTE GRANCHE店), listed in the Antenna shops and take-away chapter (page 234), has a variety of Nagoya-style kushiage skewers ready to take home or eat in the small cafeteria area next to the shop.

Data

Teppen (Otemachi) — 03-6273-4901
なかめのてっぺん 丸の内
iiyo!! B1F, Marunouchi 1-4-1, Chiyoda-ku
Open 11am-2, 5-11:30pm (LO) daily.

Rokuhara (Akasaka) — 03-3584-0698
六波羅
Akasaka 4-2-2, B1F, Minato-ku
Open 11:30am-1:30, 5:30-11pm (LO). Closed Sundays.

Tanaka (Shinjuku) — 03-6274-8594
串カツ田中 新宿3丁目店
Kumasan Bldg 1F, Shinjuku 3-12-4, Shinjuku-ku
Open 5pm-1:30am (LO) daily.

Kushinobo Bekkan (Shinjuku) — 03-3356-3865
串の坊 新宿伊勢丹会館店
Isetan Kaikan 3F, Shinjuku 3-15-17, Shinjuku-ku
Open 11:30am-3, 5-9:30pm (LO) daily.

Soba Kichi (Marunouchi) — 03-5222-5133
ソバキチ
Shin-Marunouchi Bldg 7F, Marunouchi 1-5-1, Chiyoda-ku
Open 11am-3:15am (LO) daily.

Kushiya Monogatari (Nishi-Shinjuku) — 03-5321-6166
串家物語 新宿西口大ガード店
Sunflower Bldg 5F, Nishi-Shinjuku 1-3-1, Shinjuku-ku
Open 4-10:30pm (LO) daily.

Oden

(fish cakes in broth)

おでん

Oden is a very simple dish—a collection of fish cakes, vegetables and fried-tofu items served in a bowl of kelp-based broth in which they've slowly simmered for several hours. A cold-weather dish that was once commonly served in street stalls, today it's best known as a cheap convenience-store snack, although you can find more refined versions of oden at izakaya around town, including a few that specialize in this dish.

Unlike most stewed dishes, the individual components in a bowl of oden are quite independent in terms of flavor, so generally diners order whichever pieces they like best, or simply get an assortment of the shop's most popular items. Typically these include big round chunks of stewed daikon radish, fried tofu in various shapes, fish cakes and fish balls (made from inexpensive fish), hard-boiled eggs, boiled potatoes and cabbage rolls. Strong yellow mustard is the traditional condiment.

Izakaya that serve oden sometimes offer original, more creative items, and these may be worth checking out; there will also be various side dishes to round out your meal. All in all oden is a subtle cuisine and perhaps an acquired taste, but it has its devoted fans, and its mild flavors make it a good match for sake.

Like many traditional Japanese dishes, there are major regional variations—Tokyo-style broth tends to use more soy sauce, Kansai style is lighter in flavor and color, Nagoya style has heavier miso flavors, and Shizuoka-style broth is beefier.

Vocabulary

oden	おでん	fish cakes in broth
oden moriawase	おでん盛り合わせ	preselected assortment of oden items
oden teishoku	おでん定食	oden set meal (with rice, soup and pickles)
daikon	大根・だいこん	chunks of Japanese radish
rōru kyabetsu	ロールキャベツ	cabbage roll
konnyaku	こんにゃく	translucent block of devil's-tongue starch
hanpen	はんぺん・半ぺん	fluffy white fish cake made with yam
chikuwa	ちくわ	tube-shaped fish cake
chikuwa-bu	ちくわぶ	tube-shaped wheat-gluten cake
tamago	たまご・玉子	hard-boiled egg
ganmo(doki)	がんも(どき)	fried tofu patties with bits of vegetables
fukuro	ふくろ	fried tofu bag filled with chopped vegetables
satsuma-age	さつま揚げ・薩摩揚げ	fried fish cakes
ko(n)bu	こ(ん)ぶ・昆布	kelp sheets rolled and tied into knots
gobō	ごぼう	burdock root
jagaimo	じゃが芋・じゃがいも	boiled potatoes

Konbuya (Kagurazaka)
こんぶや 神楽坂

Oden is a humble cuisine, but it reaches new heights of sophistication at Konbuya, where it's paired with well-chosen craft sake and shochu in an elegant dining room. In addition to oden you'll find a good selection of seasonal small dishes—mostly simple fare like horse-meat sashimi and fried ginkgo nuts that rely on high-quality ingredients rather than fancy recipes.

As for the main attraction—the oden menu features some three dozen individual items, ranging from typical fish balls and daikon chunks to more unusual choices like gyoza dumplings, kakuni stewed pork (wrapped in fried tofu), and grilled tarako (cod roe).

You may be tempted to just order the twelve-item moriawase menu (¥3600), but it's really worth the extra effort to peruse the menu and order a la carte—the more unusual items here are what set Konbuya apart from other oden shops. For example, the ume tsukune is a very tasty chicken-meat patty such as you'd find at a yakitoriya, livened up with a refreshing infusion of sour minced plum.

The anago no yuba-maki (grilled eel wrapped in tofu skin) is another standout, while the savory simmered apple slices make a nice finishing touch. The simpler items do provide a nice contrast—the daikon chunks are soft and succulent, delivering the konbu-rich flavor of the broth, while the hanpen is light but not bland, and pleasantly fluffy.

Note that the prices on the menu do not include tax or 10% service charge; budget around ¥4000–6000 for ample food and drink. There's no English menu, but the restaurant's website lists the current menu if you wish to study it ahead of time. The restaurant is located near the end of a narrow alleyway off Waseda-dori, around the corner from a 7-Eleven branch.

[Although most customers are in groups, there is a comfortable counter area in case you're dining solo.]

Otakō (Mitsukoshimae)
お多幸 神田店

Lunch hour is a good time to sample the oden at this long-established specialty izakaya—a teishoku (set meal) with a four-piece oden bowl plus rice, soup and pickles, is just ¥780, and there are some seventeen different items to choose from. Four pieces is just about right for a lunchtime appetite, but if you want more you can add on extra items for ¥160 each, or ¥320 for deluxe items like their special hanpen and stuffed cabbage.

The oden menu covers the usual bases—fish cakes, fish balls, fried tofu and so on—prepared in a traditional Kanto-style broth, but somehow the results here are a just a bit deeper and more flavorful than usual. The daikon radish is particularly rich, and the stuffed cabbage is pleasantly soft in texture and large in size. Tart pickled cucumber slices, sliced very thin, make a nice contrasting side dish.

In the evening the oden menu expands to 25 items, and they offer side dishes like tempura-fried fish and freshly made tofu. The small list of three or four premium sakes changes every month. The shop itself is large and old-fashioned, with a comfortable counter overlooking the simmering vats, plus a good number of tables. Otako first opened in 1912, while this branch dates back to 1971.

Budget around ¥3500 for oden, side dishes and drinks at dinnertime.

[The counter area is comfortable for solo diners, especially at lunchtime.]

Ōdako (Ueno)
大凧

Odako is notable for its selection of premium craft sake from small producers, an excellent match for the subtle flavors of the oden here. The oden itself comes in a light, Kansai-style broth; some recommended items include yuba (silky tofu skin), hotate (scallops), and the peppery ganmodoki tofu-vegetable cake.

There's also a tempting selection of creative small-dish

izakaya fare that relies heavily on seasonal vegetables. There's counter seating on two floors, although the downstairs counter might be more fun, as it offers a view of the central oden pot. The sake selection includes daily specials that may not be on the written menu, but you can ask for recommendations. Prices are very reasonable, and the shop is quite popular, so it's a good idea to call ahead or arrive early in the evening. [Most seating is at one of the restaurant's counters.]

Rakan (Yaesu)
羅かん

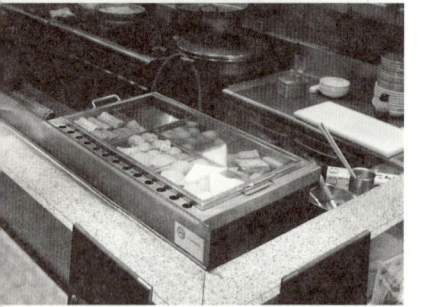

This is one of the more accessible places in town to try gourmet oden—they're open all day rather than just evenings, and the spacious counter and train-station location make it a comfortable spot for solo diners. Lunch (served until 2 pm) is an especially good deal—for ¥1200 you can get an oden-centered meal featuring six pieces of oden in broth plus sashimi, a magnificent stewed tomato, wakame soup, pickles and rice.

The oden, simmered in a mild dashi broth, is fairly typical, although the spicy fish ball was a pleasant surprise. The oden selection expands after 4:30 pm, as the subtle dashi-type oden is joined by hearty miso-stewed items like roast duck and pork tongue. Assorted platters of five oden pieces are priced at ¥1600 for miso and ¥1500 for dashi. If you want to make a night of it, there's a full menu of izakaya small dishes—sashimi, grilled fish, fried foods—along with sake and shochu. The intensely flavored, miso-based beef-tendon stew (gyusuji-nikomi) is especially recommended, and it's also available as a lunchtime set for ¥1000.

Seating is at the twelve-person counter or a big common table, both with sunken floor seating. Take your shoes off at the entrance to the restaurant.

Inagaki (Hanzōmon)
おでん割烹 稲垣

The decor and tableware at Inagaki are more stylish than your typical neighborhood izakaya, although the atmosphere is still quite down to earth, attracting a lively after-work crowd.

The oden at the heart of the menu is fairly traditional, and served in three different styles of broth—soy-flavored Kanto style, lighter Kansai style, and heavier miso-flavored Nagoya style. The smaller Nagoya menu covers eight oden items, while the main menu offers 36 different items in a choice of Kanto- or Kansai-style broth.

Some highlights include juicy scallops, very airy hanpen, nice plump oysters, and richly flavored Nagoya-style daikon chunks. Assorted sashimi of the day and traditional izakaya-style side dishes are available to supplement your oden if you're hungry.

The sake list is quite limited, and there are a few shochu

choices. Budget around ¥4000 for dinner with drinks. Inagaki doesn't take reservations, so it's a good idea to show up well before 6 pm if you want a seat. Seatings are for two and a half hours, so there may be another opportunity at around 8:30 pm. The shop is closed on weekends, and for various extended holidays like Obon and Golden Week, so phone ahead if you're not sure if they'll be open. Counter seating is available.

Excello (Shimo-Kitazawa)
Excello しずおか屋

This unusual merger of an oden shop and a soul music bar plays classic seventies soul in the background as you enjoy Shizuoka-style oden. The broth is darker and beefier than the typical Tokyo version, and the shop's "black hanpen"—a variation on the usual white and fluffy fish cake—is one of the most popular items. Budget around ¥2000–3000.

More oden

- **Surugaya Kahei** (駿河屋賀兵衛), listed in the Regional specialties chapter (page 82), serves Shizuoka-style oden along with their local seafood fare.

Data

Konbuya (Kagurazaka) — 03-5946-8988
昆布屋
Kagurazaka K Bldg 1F, Kagurazaka 3-2, Shinjuku-ku
Open 4-11pm (LO) daily.

Otakō (Mitsukoshimae) — 03-3242-0753
お多幸 神田店
Nihonbashi Muromachi 4-3-11, Chuo-ku
Open 11am-1:30, 4:30-10:30pm (LO). Closed weekends.

Ōdako (Ueno) — 03-3836-4906
大凧
Ueno 2-3-1, Taito-ku
Open 5:30-11pm daily.

Rakan (Yaesu) — 03-3287-1981
羅かん
Kurobei Yokocho (B1F), Marunouchi 1-9-1, Chiyoda-ku
Open 11am-11pm daily.

Inagaki (Hanzōmon) — 03-3230-2757
おでん割烹 稲垣
Hirakawacho 1-8-8, Chiyoda-ku
Open 5-10pm (LO). Closed weekends.

Excello (Shimo-Kitazawa) — 03-3465-6154
Excello しずおか屋
Kitazawa 2-6-6, #202, Setagaya-ku
Open 6pm-midnight. Closed Sundays.

Regional dishes and other comfort foods
ご当地グルメ

Many of the dishes and cuisines covered in this book originate in areas other than Tokyo; for example okonomiyaki is associated with Hiroshima and Osaka, grilled beef tongue is a specialty of the Sendai area, and so on. In this chapter I'll introduce a few more regional cuisines and local variations of popular dishes, and convenient places to sample them without leaving Tokyo.

Nagoya is known for several famous local dishes that definitely qualify as B-kyu cuisine—miso-coated pork cutlets, deep-fried prawns and spicy deep-fried chicken wings among them. The **Nagasaki** area of Kyushu is the home of a couple of interesting seafood-heavy noodle dishes—sara-udon (crunchy dried noodles, seafood and vegetables in a thick ankake sauce) and champon (ramen-style noodles in a soupy mix of ingredients).

In addition to the shops listed here, regional-focused

izakaya are another good place to sample local regional dishes along with local sake and shochu brands. And sometimes regional "antenna shops," discussed in a later chapter, offer local delicacies at a convenient take-out counter.

Regional dishes and other comfort foods

Chapter 1 Izakaya-style pub fare

Vocabulary

tebasaki　手羽先　chicken wings

ebi furai　エビフライ・えびフライ　deep-fried prawns

teppan tonkatsu　鉄板とんかつ　tonkatsu covered in miso sauce

sara udon　皿うどん　crisp noodles topped with seafood and vegetables in sauce

Nagasaki champon　長崎ちゃんぽん　noodles in a thick pork soup

shiokara　塩辛　fermented shellfish guts

Sekai no Yamachan (Kyobashi)
世界の山ちゃん

Discover the unique charm of Nagoya's quirky cuisine at this Tokyo outlet of a beloved Nagoya izakaya chain. The spicy chicken wings are the biggest draw here, and we'd suggest at least one order (five wings) per person; repeat as necessary. (Get the regular wings, not the "black wings" drenched in sauce.) The dote-ni—a Nagoya-esque version of motsu-nikomi—is also a standout, showcasing a variety of deeply flavored, tender pork organ meats in a rich, but not overpowering, miso-based stew.

Another popular Nagoya specialty is ebi furai (deep-fried prawns), and the ones here are quite good, prepared with a super-crunchy outer shell. If you want something more filling, the "Taiwan ramen" is a faithful rendition of another Nagoya local dish; there's not really much connection with actual Taiwanese-style noodles other than the name.

The drinks list offers a couple of local Nagoya craft sake, a miso-flavored beer, and the usual assortment of cocktails, draft beer and shochu. Budget around ¥2000–2500 for dinner with drinks. Note that this is one of the few branches of this chain with a non-smoking section. English menus are available.

Yabaton (Yaesu)
矢場とん 東京駅グランルーフ店

One of Nagoya's most famous tonkatsu shops, Yabaton is known for their tasty miso-slathered cutlets and their cute pig-sumo wrestler mascot. The teppan tonkatsu (¥1365) is their best-selling dish—a hefty portion of fatty pork cutlet covered in a sweetish miso sauce, laid over a bed of cabbage and served on a metal platter that steams and sizzles as it arrives in front of you. The large and very meaty pork soup is highly recommended as a side dish.

Jidoriya (Nakano)
ぢどり屋 中野店

The beef motsu-nikomi (organ-meat stew) here is richly flavored but delicate—the individual meats all have distinctive tastes, and blocks of tofu serve to soak up the juices of the stew. Jidoriya specializes in Hakata cuisine—cooking from the Fukuoka area of northern Kyushu—and other menu highlights include charcoal-grilled heirloom-breed chicken and deep-fried chicken skin. There's a good selection of premium sake, available in smaller tasting sizes if you want to sample and compare. An English-language menu is provided.

Konne (Nishi-Shinjuku)
Konne

Charcoal-grilled chicken, as it's prepared in Miyazaki Prefecture in southern Kyushu, has an intense charcoal flavor and is often quite chewy, being traditionally prepared using free-range chicken. You can try it for yourself in the small cafeteria section of this Miyazaki antenna shop, although the version here is less chewy than average.

It comes with a heap of shredded cabbage and a dollop of yuzu-kosho (a spicy citrus-flavored condiment) for ¥550, or as part of a set meal with pickles, soup and rice for ¥700. Other menu options include curry rice and "obiten," a type of fish cake that incorporates tofu, miso paste and brown sugar. Three kinds of craft beer come in bottles for ¥600.

Buy your food and drink tickets from the ticket machine and hand them to the person at the counter; there's an English-language menu that explains the various dishes in detail. Seating is at a communal table or at a counter facing the shop's front window. The adjoining retail shop also sells ready-to-go vacuum-packed pouches of charcoal-grilled chicken from several different producers.

Ringer Hut Shibuya South Exit (Shibuya)
リンガーハット渋谷南口店

This popular Kyushu-based chain shop is a convenient place to sample two types of Nagasaki-style noodles—sara-udon (crisp fried ramen noodles topped with vegetables, pork and seafood in a thick sauce), and Nagasaki champon (similar to sara-udon but in a thick pork-based soup). Side dishes include gyoza dumplings (regular, cheese, and mentaiko-cheese) and fried rice. The chain has several branches around town, many of them open 24 hours a day.

Fujitohachi (Akasaka)
ふじとはち

This comfortably casual izakaya showcases the food of both Yamanashi and Shizuoka Prefectures, with some nicely prepared local dishes that are usually hard to find in Tokyo. The best of these may be their version of houtou, an udon dish from the Kofu (Yamanashi) area where the broad wheat noodles are simmered in a thick, rich soup made with kabocha pumpkins and other vegetables. Also worth trying are their Hamamatsu (Shizuoka) style gyoza dumplings, which have a rather mushy pork filling and a delicious casing that's crisp on one side and soft on the other.

They also prepare a fairly representative version of Koshu (Yamanashi) style stewed chicken giblets (torimotsu nikomi). Unlike most giblet stews, this one isn't swimming in a rich broth, but comes with just a small amount of dark, strongly flavored sauce, while the individual giblets—heart, gizzard, liver, and early-stage egg—are still firm and retain their own distinctive flavors.

The menu also features a lot of bacon dishes (including bacon and eggs!), and very good grilled ray fins, softer and thicker than usual. On the drinks menu you'll find several craft sake labels (including a nice one from Shizuoka brewery Kaiun), a few craft beers, and a big selection of Koshu wines, which are attractively priced at ¥1920–2810 per bottle. Budget around ¥3000–4000 for dinner with drinks. Open until 3 am Fridays, 11 pm Saturdays. No lunch on Saturdays.

Surugaya Kahei (Akihabara)
駿河屋賀兵衛

Shiokara—aka fermented fish and shellfish guts—is a traditional sake-drinking snack, but with its rather pungent and salty character it's definitely an acquired taste. This stylish little bar may be the best place in town to try it, though. Run by a Shizuoka-based shiokara producer, Surugaya Kahei offers some thirty different varieties of this delicacy, including unusual dishes like shiokara bruschetta.

There's also a nice selection of some three dozen craft sake to explore, and a good seafood-based food menu in addition to the shiokara. Sushi made with fish marinated in yuzu kosho (a spicy citrus-pepper seasoning) is worth a try, as is the excellent grilled anago (saltwater eel). If you're stumped on what to order, the sashimi platter of the day is always reliable, and they do a nice Shizuoka-style oden.

The setting is quite charming as well—the arched, high-ceilinged space is part of a repurposed former train station from the 1950s. Budget around ¥2000–4000 in the evening for food and drink.

More regional dishes

- Freshly prepared take-out popular in various regions of Japan are sometimes sold at prefectural "antenna shops"—see the chapter on "Antenna Shops and More Takeaway" (page 228) for some suggestions.

Data

Sekai no Yamachan (Kyobashi) — 03-3277-3650
世界の山ちゃん
Heiwa Bldg #3, B1F, Kyobashi 3-3-13, Chuo-ku
Open 5-11:30pm (LO) daily.

Yabaton (Yaesu) — 03-3212-8810
矢場とん 東京駅グランルーフ店
Tokyo Gran Roof B1F, Marunouchi 1-9-1, Chiyoda-ku
Open 10am-10pm (LO) daily.

Jidoriya (Nakano) — 03-3388-7447
ぢどり屋 中野店
Nakano 5-59-1, Nakano-ku
Open 4pm-12:30am (Sat, Sun 12-) daily.

Konne (Nishi-Shinjuku) — 03-5333-7764
Konne
Southern Terrace, Yoyogi 2-2-1, Shibuya-ku
Open 11am-9pm daily.

Ringer Hut Shibuya South Exit (Shibuya) — 03-3464-0668
リンガーハット渋谷南口店
Sakuragaokacho 2-12, Shibuya-ku
Open 10am-5am daily.

Fujitohachi (Akasaka) — 030-6277-6614
ふじとはち
Akasaka 5-1-5, Minato-ku
Open 11:30am-2, 5pm-midnight. Closed Sundays.

Surugaya Kahei (Akihabara) — 03-5295-0310
駿河屋賀兵衛
Maach Ecute 1F, Kanda Sudacho 1-25-4, Chiyoda-ku
Open 11am-11pm daily.

Chapter 2

Budget meals

お手頃メニュー

Online Map
bento.com/maps/budget.html

Tonkatsu

(pork cutlet)

豚カツ

Tonkatsu is one of Japan's most popular comfort foods. It's made by cutting pork fillets into thick slices that are heavily breaded and slowly deep-fried. The preparation is simple in concept, but getting just the right balance of batter and breading, frying temperature and cooking length is a real art, and when it's done well the result is a juicy, delicious slab of pork encased in a beautifully crisp, ungreasy coating.

Over the past decade or so there has been a boom in premium pork brands—often from heirloom and newly devloped hybrid breeds—that in many ways rivals the interest in premium wagyu beef. Taking advantage of this interest, many long-running tonkatsu shops have stepped up their game in recent years and now offer one or more premium-brand alternatives to their regular pork cutlets.

Cutlets at tonkatsu shops are generally available in two different cuts—"rosu," a somewhat fatty loin of pork, and "hire," a leaner tenderloin cut from which the fat has been trimmed. Whatever your feelings about fatty meats, it's worth trying both to see which you like better. Another popular item is "menchi katsu," a ground-pork patty that tends to be much juicier than a regular cutlet. Menus may also offer deep-fried prawns, potato and crab croquettes, and "mixed-fry" platters.

Tonkatsu is served as the centerpiece of a set teishoku meal, which includes rice, pickles, heaps of shredded cabbage, and soup—often a pork-based soup called "tonjiru" rather than miso soup. Condiments typically include strong mustard, salad dressing for your cabbage, salt, lemon, and tonkatsu sauce, a thicker version of Worcestershire sauce. Established shops often develop their own exclusive recipes for salad dressing and tonkatsu sauce, and sometimes there's more than one tonkatsu sauce to choose from.

Vocabulary

tonkatsu　とんかつ　pork cutlet

rōsu katsu　ロースかつ　fatty loin of pork

hire katsu　ひれかつ・ヒレかつ　lean tenderloin pork

jō hire katsu　上ヒレかつ　deluxe lean tenderloin pork

menchi katsu　メンチカツ　ground-pork patty

kurobuta　黒豚　premium Berkshire pork

korokke　コロッケ　croquettes (usually crab or potato)

ebi furai　エビフライ　deep-fried prawns

mikkusu furai　ミックスフライ　mixed-fry platter

Agezuki (Kagurazaka)
あげづき

Located in an attractively furnished Kagurazaka basement, walls decorated with colorful sake and shochu bottles, Agezuki feels more like an upscale izakaya than a tonkatsu shop. And indeed they offer a well-curated list of more than a dozen craft sakes, in either standard 1-go flasks or 65 ml tasting sizes, along with sake-appropriate snacks. Several types of shochu, a few inexpensive wines and the usual beer round out the drinks options.

Tonkatsu is still the main draw, of course, and the cutlet here is first-rate, made from a hybrid breed of pork sourced from a small farm in Miyazaki, Kyushu. The pork is fried in a mixture of imported Dutch lard and vegetable oils, resulting in a light-colored, thin but flaky crust. Diners are encouraged to try their first bite of cutlet with salt alone, to savor the rich and pleasantly fatty flavor without sauce. Bowls of tasty pickles are supplied on each table.

Dinnertime main dishes include the usual rosu, hire and menchi cutlets, as well as ginger-pork, chicken, prawns and Hokkaido scallops. Mains can be ordered a la carte or as part of a teishoku set with soup, pickles, rice and a dab of potato salad.

Lunches are priced from ¥1100, with four options including

pork rosu and chicken breast. Note that in spite of the posted closing time of 2 pm, they often finish their quota of lunch tonkatsu at around 1 pm, so it's recommended that you show up early and wait on line. Likewise, reservations are a good idea in the evening.

Butagumi Shokudo (Roppongi Hills)
豚組食堂

Nishi-Azabu pork specialist Butagumi raised the bar on tonkatsu with their five-pork tasting platters showcasing a rotating selection of domestic and imported premium pork varieties. This is a newer, more accessible branch of Butagumi—it's actually a bit nicer than the main branch—and it's an excellent place to explore some of these premium-grade heirloom breeds of pork.

Regular tonkatsu set meals start at around ¥1000, while more exotic hybrid meats with names like "Golden Boar" range from ¥2500–3000. The spacious counter surrounds an open kitchen area where you can watch your tonkatsu being prepared.

Narikura (Takadanobaba)
成蔵

Four or five different heirloom breeds of pork are generally on offer here, with dinnertime teishoku set meals starting at around

¥1400–2000 depending on the type of pork. The teishoku comes with a deep, richly porky tonjiru soup (¥100 if you want a refill) and tasty potato salad and pickles. The pork is covered in a light-colored coating that's flakier than average, with a good balance of meat to fat.

There's space for around twenty in the pleasant basement dining room, and the shop fills up fast—there's often a line soon after dinnertime opening hour. Drinks include Ebisu beer and inexpensive wine by the glass.

Takeda (Yotsuya)
かつれつ四谷たけだ

This lively neighborhood shop does a brisk business both day and night, so try to avoid peak lunch and dinner hours if you don't want to wait. In addition to doing excellent tonkatsu, in both regular and premium grades, the kitchen also turns out deep-fried prawns, oysters, fish and chicken. One of the most popular items is a combo platter of menchi-katsu (ground-pork patties) and croquettes.

The mochi-buta rosu (¥1350) features a fatty cutlet made from mochi-buta pork, a hybrid breed developed in Tohoku for its rich flavor. The breading is a medium golden brown, slightly thick and soft in texture rather than crunchy.

The waitress suggested trying it with coarse salt, and the cutlet turned out to be extremely succulent and tasty without the usual tonkatsu sauce. The goma-dare (sesame dressing) on the counter will perk up your shredded cabbage. Drinks include budget wines by the glass as well as bottled beer.

Katsukura (Shinjuku)
かつくら 新宿高島屋店

This central Tokyo branch of a popular Kyoto-based tonkatsu shop stands out for both its overall high quality and the breadth of its menu offerings. In addition to regular and premium-pork grades of tonkatsu they offer dishes like deep-fried scallops and prawns, and yuba (tofu-skin) croquettes.

You'll find a wealth of side dishes like chawanmushi, tofu salad, and kakuni stewed pork, and there's a bewildering choice of set meals assembled from various permutations of dishes. The drinks selection is better than average, with a few nice sake brands. The decor is tasteful and modern. All in all, Katsukura is a reliable standby when you're in the mood for tonkatsu.

Hirata Bokujō (Nihonbashi)
平田牧場

The gourmet tonkatsu here is made from tasty premium hybrid pork from a small farm in Yamagata. Pickles, side dishes and even the rice are all fancier than average, and you can grind your own fresh sesame seeds to add to your tonkatsu sauce. Tonkatsu set meals are priced ¥1400–2500 at dinnertime, while lunch starts at ¥1000.

Manpei (Awajicho)
とんかつ 万平

Highly rated by Tokyo's tonkatsu cognoscenti, the cutlet here sports a thin but pleasantly crunchy coating and juicy meat on the inside, the result of being briefly oven-baked after it's fried. It's served with a scrumptious tofu soup. Other menu options include sauteed pork, menchi katsu and fried oysters in season.

The brightly lit, austere setting at this long-running shop

might make it a better choice for a quick lunch rather than dinner. All seating is at tables for four, so you might have to share when they're crowded. Teishoku are priced at ¥1650 for rosu-katsu and ¥1950 for hire-katsu.

[On Saturdays they serve lunch only, no dinner.]

Data

Agezuki (Kagurazaka) — 03-6265-0029
あげづき

Yamanouchi Bldg B1F, Kagurazaka 3-2, Shinjuku-ku

Open 11:30am-2:30, 6-10pm (LO). Closed Tues, 3rd Wed.

Butagumi Shokudo (Roppongi Hills) — 03-3408-6751
豚組食堂

Roppongi Hills North Tower B1F, Roppongi 6-2-31, Minato-ku

Open 11am-10:30pm (LO) daily.

Narikura (Takadanobaba) — 03-6380-3823
成蔵

Ozawa Bldg B1F, Takadanobaba 1-32-11, Shinjuku-ku

Open 11am-2, 5:30-9pm (LO). Closed Thursdays.

Takeda (Yotsuya) — 03-3357-6004
かつれつ四谷たけだ

Yotsuya 1-4-2, Shinjuku-ku

Open 11am-3, 5-9pm (LO). Closed Sundays.

Katsukura (Shinjuku) — 03-5361-1878
かつくら 新宿高島屋店

Times Square 14F, Sendagaya 5-24-2, Shibuya-ku

Open 11am-10pm (LO) daily.

Hirata Bokujō (Nihonbashi) — 03-6214-3129
平田牧場

Coredo Nihonbashi 4F, Nihonbashi 1-4-1, Chuo-ku

Open 11am-2:30, 5-10pm (LO) daily.

Manpei (Awajicho) — 03-3251-4996
とんかつ 万平

Kanda Sudacho 1-11, Chiyoda-ku

Open 11:30am-2, 5:30-7pm. Closed Sundays and holidays.

Gyūkatsu

(beef cutlet)

牛カツ

Gyukatsu is a popular new arrival Tokyo's culinary scene. It's currently served in only a few specialty shops and izakaya, but it's already drawing crowds, long lines and TV coverage.

Gyukatsu is basically a bovine version of tonkatsu (pork cutlet); the meat is prepared rare in the middle, with a crunchy breaded coating, and served with wasabi and soy sauce, salt, and various other sauces. Tororo (grated yam) is usually offered as an optional dip.

Most gyukatsu shops are very informal counter-style restaurants that serve teishoku set meals with barley rice, soup, pickles and shredded cabbage. Double-size portions of meat are a popular add-on.

Vocabulary

gyūkatsu 牛かつ deep-fried beef cutlet
teishoku 定食 set meal, with rice, soup and pickles
tororo とろろ grated yam
(daikon) oroshi (大根)おろし grated daikon radish
menchi katsu メンチかつ minced (beef) cutlet

Asakusa Gyūkatsu (Asakusa)
浅草牛かつ

This tiny, nine-seat counter shop just may serve the best gyukatsu in Tokyo. The meat is beautifully marbled, encased in a thin, softly crunchy coating and quite tasty with just a bit of grated rock salt. Do try the onion sauce, though—this is also one of the best in town, assertively pungent with a bit of kick to it.

The spicy pickles are outstanding; my only complaint was that there weren't more of them. The teishoku set with a double order of meat (260g; ¥1900) is recommended, although they also sell triple and quadruple meat options. Grated yam is an extra ¥100 if you like that sort of thing. Menus are in English and Korean, and there's a detailed instruction sheet on how to eat.

Katchan (Jimbocho)
勝ちゃん

Katchan serves a unique, very tasty dipping sauce for their gyukatsu—it's both spicy and sweet, and it really brings out the flavor of the meat. The recommended dish here is the double-size portion of gyukatsu (beef cutlet) with menchi katsu (deep-fried minced-meat patty) on the side, a bargain at just ¥1180. The beef is tender and served rare in the middle, and the menchi katsu is the perfect counterpoint—very juicy with lots of onion bits adding texture and flavor, wrapped in a crunchy fried shell.

Gyukatsu is available in single, double and triple servings, with optional grated yam (tororo) or grated daikon radish (oroshi) toppings for an extra ¥100 or so. Purchase a ticket for your meal from the ticket machine at the door when you arrive. No dinner on Saturdays.

Ippoippo (Yotsuya)
一歩一歩

Unlike the usual counter-style restaurants that specialize in gyukatsu, Ippoippo is a full-fledged izakaya. The lunchtime menu, though, has just a single item—gyukatsu teishoku. It's a nice version too, properly rare in the middle, crunchy on the outside, with a bit more fat than usual, to add some extra flavor. Salt, ponzu and soy sauce are provided for dipping, along with a mound of wasabi. The side dish—fried tofu ball with vegetables—helps make this a well-balanced meal.

At night gyukatsu is served a la carte, and the menu expands to offer kushiage skewers and other deep-fried delights, along with sashimi and izakaya-style side dishes. Kushiage ranges from ¥100–250 per piece, and it's well prepared, the coating crunchy and free of oiliness, the vegetables crisp and fresh-tasting. The intensely flavored, miso-based motsu-nikomi (beef organ-meat stew) is also worth a try.

There are six sake to choose from, including special seasonal brews, along with shochu and beer. Budget around ¥3000–4000 in the evening, ¥1000 at lunch.

Motomura (Shinjuku)
牛かつ もと村

There are lines to get into Motomura day and night, and it's easy to understand why once you've tasted their very popular gyukatsu. Served rare in the middle with a thin, crunchy layer of breading around it, the lightly marbled beef is tender and very flavorful. Season it to taste with rock salt, pepper, onion sauce, soy sauce and wasabi.

One selling point of Motomura is that they provide each table or counter space with a small hibachi, so you can finish off, or at least heat up, individual slices of cutlet. Since the thinly sliced meat tends to cool off very quickly on the plate, this is a welcome touch.

A single portion of beef, with a set meal of rice, soup, potato salad, cabbage and pickles, is ¥1200; add an extra ¥700 for a double-sized portion of beef, and ¥100 for a side dish of grated yam for dipping. No reservations or credit cards; English-language menus are available, along with detailed instructions on how to eat your gyukatsu. (There are also branches in Shibuya and Yaesu.)

Iroha (Ikebukuro)
牛かつ いろは

The gyukatsu here is covered with a thin, crunchy coating that softens quickly when dipped in sauce. Like their competitor Motomura, Iroha supplies each diner with a miniature brazier with which to heat up individual slices of beef that may have cooled off on the plate. The meat is quite tasty after ten seconds on the grill and a brief dip in freshly ground salt, but a splash of the intensely flavored onion sauce makes it even better.

As usual, Iroha's cutlet comes as part of a set meal, here with tororo (grated yam), rice, rather mild pickles, soup, shredded cabbage and a dollop of potato salad. You can vary the size of your meat portion from 100g to 230g or more, and you can leave out the yam (say "tororo nashi") to save ¥100. A standard 130g portion without tororo is ¥1300.

The small basement shop has eight rather tightly packed counter seats and another six at tables. There may be a line at peak hours, but usually not in midafternoon.

Katsugyū (Ogawamachi)
京都勝牛

The gyukatsu at this Kyoto-based shop has a nice thick, crunchy coating, and the beef has a decent amount of fat attached to it, but somehow the flavor of the meat itself is more subtle and less assertive than average. Condiments include the usual wasabi, a salt and pepper mix (probably the best match), an original sauce, soy sauce, and a curry-flavored dip that's tasty but somewhat overpowering.

The cutlet comes in three different sizes (100g, 130g, and 160g portions of meat), ranging roughly from ¥1080–1580, with a premium Angus wagyu option priced at ¥1980. The set meal includes barley rice and a salty Kyoto-style miso soup, but no pickles, unfortunately. The decor of the dining area is upscale fast-food restaurant, with mostly counter seating plus a few small tables. The refrigerated case in the window full of aging slabs of beef helps to set the mood.

There's also a branch in Akihabara, on the restaurant floor of Yodobashi Camera (03-3251-0090).

Aona (Takadanobaba)
あおな 高田馬場店

The beef cutlet here has a lovely, extra-crunchy coating, and it's accompanied by a well-constructed vegetable salad and a tasty, peppery soup. Condiments include artisanal rock salt and oil with red pepper, and for an extra ¥100 you can order a knob of fresh wasabi and a grinder.

The meat itself can be chewier than

average, although the premium beef options (Angus beef and marbled Angus beef) may be more tender. The menchi katsu (deep-fried minced-beef patty) is another option. Set menus start at ¥1250.

Data

Asakusa Gyūkatsu (Asakusa) — 03-3842-1800
浅草牛かつ
Kaminarimon Uemura Bldg B1F, Kaminarimon 2-17-10, Taito-ku
Open 11am-10:30pm (LO; Sat -9:30, Sun -8:30) daily.

Katchan (Jimbocho) — 03-5577-6050
勝ちゃん
Kanda Jimbocho 1-8, Chiyoda-ku
Open 11am-3:30, 5-10:30pm. Closed Sundays.

Ippoippo (Yotsuya) — 03-6273-1669
一歩一歩
Koizumi Bldg B1F, Yotsuya 1-20, Shinjuku-ku
Open 11:30am-2, 5-10pm (LO). Closed Sundays.

Motomura (Shinjuku) — 03-3354-0171
牛かつ もと村
Shinjuku 3-32-2 B1F, Shinjuku-ku
Open 11am-10pm daily.

Iroha (Ikebukuro) — 03-3971-2838
牛かつ いろは
Tomoaki Bldg B1F, Higashi-Ikebukuro 1-9-7, Toshima-ku
Open 11am-10pm (LO) daily.

Katsugyū (Ogawamachi) — 03-3292-7802
京都勝牛
Chiyoda 21 Bldg 1F, Kanda Mitoshirocho 9-7, Chiyoda-ku
Open 11am-9:30pm (LO) daily.

Aona (Takadanobaba) — 03-6908-9779
あおな 高田馬場店
Takadanobaba 3-2-5, Shinjuku-ku
Open 11:30am-10:30pm daily.

Okonomiyaki and Monjayaki

(savory pancakes)

お好み焼き、もんじゃ焼き

Okonomiyaki is a casual, fun dish that's quite popular with foreign visitors to Japan. It's basically a savory pancake made with seafood, pork, cabbage and other vegetables, cooked on a flat grill and dressed with mayonnaise and tangy sauce. The "okonomi" part of the name means "what you like," and customers can choose their own favorite ingredients to add to their pancakes. Many shops have customers cook their own okonomiyaki at the table.

Regional styles
This is a dish with very distinct regional variations. In Osaka-style okonomiyaki, all the component ingredients are mixed together in a bowl of batter, then spread out on the grill for cooking. The Hiroshima version is more complicated and takes longer to prepare, as the chef (not the customer) assembles distinct layers of toppings, vegetables, noodles,

fried egg and pancake base into the final product.

Finally, there's a version called monjayaki, which is similar to Osaka style but with a thinner, runnier batter. Monjayaki is generally found only in the Tokyo area, particularly in the Tokyo Bay neighborhood of Tsukishima, which is home to dozens of monjayaki restaurants clustered together in one small zone.

Ordering, cooking and eating
If you're in a cook-it-yourself shop, once you've decided on your main ingredient (e.g., pork, shrimp or squid) and your optional fillings, the waiter will turn on the grill at your table, brush on some oil, and deliver a bowl with the batter and ingredients. Mix these together and pour the mixture onto the grill (once it's hot enough), then use a spatula to turn over your pancake when it's ready. Note that this might

take a bit longer than you would expect; ask your waiter for advice if you're not sure, or watch what other diners are doing. If there's an option for the waiter or chef to cook your okonomiyaki, you might want to take them up on their offer unless you're feeling adventurous.

If you're in a Hiroshima-style shop, the ordering process is a bit different—in addition to choosing ingredients like shrimp and squid, you'll generally have an option of either "soba" noodles (actually thin ramen-style wheat noodles) or thicker udon noodles. There may also be an option for no noodles at all. The chef will prepare your pancake and serve it on the grill in front of you. Cut the pancake into bite-size rectangles, and add extra sauce, mayonnaise and other condiments to taste as you eat.

The metal grill in an okonomiyaki restaurant is called a teppan, and menus will feature other foods prepared on the teppan grill, such as yakisoba (stir-fried ramen-style noodles with vegetables and sauce) and grilled seafood, vegetables and meat. Many shops have one large teppan grill with a counter surrounding it (a good place to watch the chefs in action), while others have separate grills at each table.

Vocabulary

okonomiyaki お好み焼き savory okonomiyaki pancakes

monjayaki もんじゃ焼き savory monjayaki pancakes

hiroshima-yaki 広島焼 Hiroshima-style (okonomiyaki)

-ten 天 okonomiyaki-style (e.g., ebi-ten: shrimp okonomiyaki)

-tama 玉 okonomiyaki-style with egg

modan-yaki モダン焼 okonomiyaki with yakisoba

soba そば thin, wheat ramen noodles

udon うどん thick, wheat udon noodles

yakisoba 焼きそば fried ramen noodles

ebi えび・海老 shrimp

ika いか squid

hotate 帆立・ホタテ scallop

buta 豚 pork

gyū 牛 beef

ninniku にんにく garlic

chiizu チーズ cheese

negi ねぎ・葱 leek

Kurumi (Kagurazaka)
くるみ

Hiroshima-style okonomiyaki is the specialty at this friendly neighborhood spot, along with a good assortment of vegetables from the teppan grill. Choose from seven or eight okonomiyaki variations, all made with a base of pork, eggs, cabbage and other vegetables, plus your choice of ramen (aka "soba") or udon noodles. In case you're extra-hungry, we were told that the ramen noodles create a more voluminous final product.

The deluxe seafood version (¥1300) incorporates shrimp, squid and scallops, all of them very tasty. Other choices include tomato-cheese, togarashi (hot peppers), and a noodle-less version. There are also more than a dozen optional fillings to choose from, including kimchee, natto, cheese and extra pork. If you want to make a night of it you can add on grilled side dishes like eringi mushrooms with bacon, or grilled chicken neck with asparagus and black pepper.

Most seating is at a big counter wrapping around the grill area, so your okonomiyaki can be served on the hot grill directly in front of you. Adding to the down-home feel, there's a fresh vegetable and fruit stand set up in front of the shop. Budget around ¥1000 for okonomiyaki, or ¥2000–2500 for a bigger dinner with drinks. Note that the lunchtime menu is a bit more limited than at dinnertime, but also a couple hundred yen cheaper.

Sanshō (Ginza)
三匠

If you've got a hearty appetite, the Special Sansho Okonomiyaki (¥1660) is the way to go—it's packed with plenty of shrimp and squid, pork, vegetables and ramen noodles, and topped with two juicy fried oysters. Sitting at the counter, you can watch the rather complicated assembly process step by step—it's quite impressive.

The finished product is nicely balanced in flavor and texture, from the thin layer of fried egg on top to the lightly charred bits of squid and the partially crunchy noodles. You can fine-tune your experience with tangy sauce, spicy mayonnaise, red pepper, black pepper and garlic powder, or order toasted garlic chips as an optional topping.

As is typical for an okonomiyaki shop, there's also a selection of other items from the teppan grill—in this case bacon-asparagus stir-fry, pork-kimchee, squid tentacles, moyashi (bean sprouts), steaks and several oyster dishes. You can choose from a selection of premium Hiroshima sake and shochu to wash it down. English menus are available.

Sansho is located on the second floor of the Hiroshima Prefecture "antenna shop," which also carries fresh produce, prepared foods, sake, wine and handicrafts from Hiroshima. Also on the second floor is a standing bar where you can sample Hiroshima sake and wine by the glass.

Carp (Kanda)
カープ 東京支店

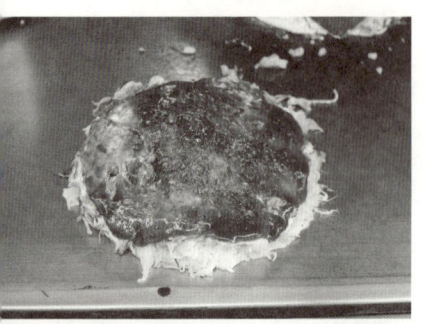

Named after Hiroshima's baseball team, this brightly lit, old-fashioned shop serves Hiroshima-style okonomiyaki all day long. You can choose from ramen ("soba") or udon noodles, with a few optional toppings like garlic cloves, squid, shrimp, cheese and corn, all displayed on hand-written menus on the wall.

The okonomiyaki here is constructed with precision, with distinct layers of egg (a bit thicker than average), noodles, bacon and other fillings, then a good volume of shredded cabbage on top of a sturdy, chewy base. Budget around ¥1000–1500 for food.

Kyochabana (Shinjuku)
京ちゃばな

Original-recipe Kyoto-style okonomiyaki (similar to Osaka-style) is the specialty of the house here, with some offbeat variations built around avocados and tomatoes. Optional toppings like pork, shrimp, cheese, bacon and mushrooms are ready to add to the mix, and the voluminous portions are big enough to share, especially if you've had starters.

Kyochabana's yakisoba is also recommended—real buckwheat noodles, rather than the usual ramen-style wheat noodles, are cooked up on the flat grill along with tomatoes and other vegetables, then livened up with tiny dabs of wasabi for an appealingly different take on this usually mundane dish. The creative side dishes are also impressive—Kyoto-style heirloom vegetables served with a tangy miso dip; sweet-potato vichyssoise; and a nice thick daikon radish steak served with yuzu and leek.

Drinks include budget wines as well as beer, shochu and plum wines. The basement dining room is cozy and unpretentious, service is friendly, and prices are quite reasonable—a nice combination in this often-overpriced neighborhood. Budget around ¥2500–3000 for dinner with a few drinks.

Sakuratei (Harajuku)
さくら亭

Attached to an experimental art gallery called Design Festa, Sakuratei is definitely the most artsy okonomiyaki shop in town, and it attracts a young Bohemian-leaning crowd. The menu offers some fifteen variations on Osaka-style okonomiyaki as well as

Tokyo-style monjayaki, yakisoba, and yaki-udon noodles.

The Kurobuta Okonomiyaki is studded with nice big chunks of Berkshire pork, and the pancake batter is made with water that was used for cooking soba noodles at a nearby soba shop. There are numerous side dishes from the teppan grill like home-made bacon and seasonal vegetables, and for dessert you can choose from five types of gelato or Taiwanese-style mango kakigori (shaved ice).

(Lunch is served until 3 pm.)

Oshio (Tsukishima)
おしお 和店

Located in the middle of Tsukushima's bustling monjayaki district, Oshio is a comfortable place to try out this local Tokyo version of okonomiyaki. The large menu includes dozens of entertaining variations such as spinach-tomato, spicy Chinese tofu, and mentaiko (cod roe) with cheese, as well as teppan-grilled salmon and scallops. Monjayaki is ¥1000–1300.

Data

Kurumi (Kagurazaka) 03-3269-4456
くるみ
Kagurazaka 5-30, Shinjuku-ku
Open 11:30am-2, 5:30-10:30pm (LO). Closed Tuesdays.

Sanshō (Ginza) 050-3774-4402
三匠
Ginza 1-6-10, Chuo-ku
Open 11am-9pm (LO) daily.

Carp (Kanda) 03-5296-0080
カープ 東京支店
Kanda Kajicho 3-5, Chiyoda-ku
Open 11am-9:30pm (LO; Sat -8pm). Closed Sundays, Mondays.

Kyochabana (Shinjuku) 03-3353-1575
京ちゃばな
Yamaguchi Bldg B1F, Shinjuku 3-6-9, Shinjuku-ku
Open 5-10:30pm (LO) daily.

Sakuratei (Harajuku) 03-3479-0039
さくら亭
Jingumae 3-20-1, Shibuya-ku
Open 11am-11pm daily.

Oshio (Tsukishima) 03-3532-9000
おしお 和店
Tsukishima 1-21-5, Chuo-ku
Open noon-10pm (LO) daily.

Udon and Curry udon

(wheat noodles)

うどん、カレーうどん

Udon noodles have long been a staple of soba shops and udon specialty shops—the thick, chewy wheat-flour noodles are served in the same manner as soba noodles, in hot broth with traditional ingredients such as leeks, fried tofu and tempura-fried shrimp.

Perhaps more interesting to the B-kyu gourmet though, is curry udon. Here the noodles are served in a bowl of curry-flavored soup, with a huge choice of add-on ingredients ranging from cheese and garlic chips to fried bananas and oysters. It turns out that the rather plain-tasting noodles make a great delivery vehicle for rich curry flavors, while the typical deep-fried toppings provide a very satisfying contrast in texture with the soup and noodles.

The wide choice of ingredients allows for endless customization of your bowl, one reason for this dish's appeal. A major drawback, though, is that curry udon is quite messy to eat, so restaurants customarily provide diners with a disposable paper bib to reduce the level of soup splatter on clothing.

    Instead of curry soup, some fusion-oriented udon shops offer other interesting variations such as Italian-style pasta sauces and ingredients. Curry udon shops generally charge similar prices for lunch and dinner, and often stay open for business all afternoon.

Vocabulary

udon	うどん	udon (wheat) noodles
karē udon	カレーうどん	udon noodles in curry soup
tsukemen	つけめん	noodles with dipping sauce
chiizu	チーズ	cheese

Anpuku (Toranomon)
あんぷく

Novel, fusion-style udon is the specialty here, with intriguing choices such as udon carbonara and beef-tendon curry udon. Recommendations include a very refined, Chinese-inspired tantanmen udon with a satisfyingly spicy sesame sauce, and a compelling Italian-style four-cheese udon that had me scooping up the very last of the sauce from the bowl.

A serving of udon here is filling enough to make a complete meal, but if you're in the mood for starters you'll find a good selection of charcoal-grilled meats, fish and vegetables. There are also original dishes like "caprese tempura"—mozzarella, cherry tomatoes and basil, tempura-fried with a light, delicate coating.

Another uniquely appealing feature at Anpuku is the small sake bar at the front of the shop. A couple dozen well-chosen craft sakes from around the country are served in taster-size 60ml or full 120ml portions, in your choice of standard sake cups or proper wine glasses (the latter is recommended). Of course you can order sake in the restaurant proper, or noodles at the sake bar as you wish. Most udon bowls are in the ¥1000–1200 range, and sake tastings are quite reasonable as well.

Nanakura (Shimbashi)
七蔵

Originally just a small counter shop serving udon noodles, Nanakura has since grown into a full-sized, lively after-work izakaya with a focus on fresh seafood. The excellent, rather unique udon noodles are still a big draw, though, and worth a special trip on their own. The udon here is served with a rich, fatty, very tasty duck-based dipping sauce with shimeji mushrooms and scallions. The noodles are thinly cut, the better to deliver the delicious sauce.

 Udon comes in three sizes (¥1080–1480), and for an extra ¥490 you can add on a mini-donburi bowl of maguro or ikura over rice. Other menu highlights include a reliable sashimi moriawase and sake-marinated grilled otoro tuna. There's a small but serviceable sake selection, and of course beer and shochu cocktails. Budget around ¥3500–4000 in the evening, or less if you just want udon.

Atsumaru (Ogawamachi)
アツマル

While the relatively unspicy curry udon noodles are the main seller here, the kitchen also turns out several other hot and cold varieties such as spicy natto, Chinese-style tantanmen, and ume-kitsune (fried tofu). The Italian-influenced cold tomato and cheese udon (¥1000) is a refreshing, rather unique bowl, with lots of fresh vegetables like turnips, mushrooms and pumpkin complementing the pleasantly chewy noodles.

The atmosphere is relaxed, and the tasteful decor—tan stucco walls, distressed concrete floor, heavy dark wooden tables—makes this seem more like a chic neighborhood cafe than a noodle joint.

Sangokuichi Island Tower (Nishi-Shinjuku)
三国一 アイランドイッツ店

Houtou is a hearty winter udon-noodle dish from the mountainous Kofu area of Yamanashi Prefecture, and this is one of the few places in Tokyo where you can find it. The houtou served here is quite substantial, loaded with chunks of chicken, pumpkin, leeks, mushrooms and other vegetables in a thick broth—a filling meal for just ¥1000.

Sangokuichi also offers a couple dozen other types of udon, including oddball "salad udon" bowls such as tuna salad and tomato salad. Drinks include a dozen different shochu and seven craft sakes (although these aren't listed on the English menu). There's also a good amount of izakaya fare—sashimi, grilled fish and side dishes—if you want more than just noodles.

Norabutaya (Yotsuya 3-chome)
のら豚屋 新宿通四谷店

The roux at this curry-udon shop is dark brown in color and spicy, with a typical flavor profile that approaches the Platonic ideal of Japanese curry. There's a bowl of thick, syrupy spicy sauce on the table if you want to add some extra heat. But what makes Norabutaya stand out from the crowd is the quirky selection of toppings that accompany the udon noodles—grilled chicken, chicken tempura, cheese, potato croquettes, and fried oysters among them.

Perhaps the most appealing is the "toro toro buta"—fatty grilled pork cheeks with a nice smoky flavor. Thin slivers of pungent scallion create a good counterpoint to the rich flavors of the curry. The noodles themselves are thick and plain, functioning mainly as a delivery vehicle for the sauce.

Curry udon starts at ¥723, with various permutations of topping ingredients available in set combinations or a la carte. The menu also offers curry rice, katsu curry rice, takoyaki and chicken karaage, the latter two as inexpensive side dishes. The interior has a rustic decor, with heavy dark-brown wooden furnishings. Most of the menu is also ready for take-out.

Senkichi (Omotesando)
千吉

A popular all-day budget chain, Senkichi offers dozens of varieties of curry udon, with dozens more optional toppings. The "creative" curry here is golden yellow in color and seems to be inspired by Vietnamese cuisine. It goes well with the optional tempura-fried shrimp kakiage, which gradually soaks up the intense curry flavors as the crunchy bits crumble into the soup. Cheese and toasted garlic toppings also enhance the curry experience.

Senkichi also offers "standard" curry udon in several variations—red, spicy, tomato—as well as tsukemen-style dipping sauces and a good number of seasonal specials. The decor has the feel of an upmarket fast-food restaurant, with a non-smoking section in front.

Senkichi (Minami-Shinjuku)
千吉

Like its Omotesando branch (see above), this budget chain offers a full range of curry udon variations to choose from. Most are priced ¥700–800 per bowl, which includes a small portion of rice and pickles on the side.

Konaya (Marunouchi)
古奈屋

This Tokyo-based chain serves a relatively spicy curry-flavored bowl of udon noodles with a small but appealing selection of toppings. Plump tempura-fried prawn is probably the most popular of these; other options include banana tempura, fried tofu, cheese, and mochi (rice cakes) toppings, tsukemen dipping noodles, or an Indian-influenced keema curry udon with minced chicken and pork.

The udon noodles themselves are quite flavorful, and thin slivers of crisp green beans in the bowl provide pleasantly contrasting texture. If you're not in a curry mood, you can choose from more traditional-style regular udon, and if you're not in an udon mood at all you can get curry rice. The dining area is simple but modern in feel, with counters looking out over the building's six-story atrium.

More udon

- **Fujitohachi** (ふじとはち), listed in the Regional specialties chapter (page 81), serves houtou udon, a specialty of the Kofu area of Yamanashi Prefecture.

Data

Anpuku (Toranomon) — 03-6257-3850
あんぷく
Toranomon Hills 4F, Toranomon 1-26, Minato-ku
Open 11am-2:30, 5-10:30pm (LO) daily.

Nanakura (Shimbashi) — 03-3571-5012
七蔵
Shimbashi Ekimae Bldg #1 2F, Shimbashi 2-20-15, Minato-ku
Open 11:20am-2:10, 5-9pm (LO). Closed weekends.

Atsumaru (Ogawamachi) — 03-3292-1444
アツマル
Kanda Suragadai 3-5, Chiyoda-ku
Open 11:30am-2:30, 5:30-8pm. Closed Sundays, 3rd Sat.

Sangokuichi Island Tower (Nishi-Shinjuku) — 03-3346-3591
三国一 アイランドイッツ店
I-Land Tower B1F, Nishi-Shinjuku 6-5-1, Shinjuku-ku
Open 11am-10:30pm (LO; Sat -10, Sun -9:30) daily.

Norabutaya (Yotsuya 3-chome) — 03-5367-2133
のら豚屋 新宿通四谷店
Ōmura Bldg 1F, Yotsuya 2-11, Shinjuku-ku
Open 11am-2:30, 5-10:30pm (LO) daily.

Senkichi (Omotesando) — 03-3400-4920
千吉
Minami-Aoyama 5-6-25, Minato-ku
Open 11am-3am daily.

Senkichi (Minami-Shinjuku) — 03-5358-7054
千吉
Yu-wa Bldg 1F, Yoyogi 2-13-6, Shibuya-ku
Open 11am-11pm daily.

Konaya (Marunouchi) — 03-5220-5500
古奈屋
Marunouchi Oazo 5F, Marunouchi 1-6-4, Chiyoda-ku
Open 11am-10:30pm (LO) daily.

Rāmen

ラーメン

Ramen is probably the most famous of Japan's backstreet "B-kyu" cuisines. Starting with a simple Chinese dish of soup and noodles, Japanese chefs focused on the soup, making it the center of attention. The noodles and toppings followed suit, and modern-day ramen is a bowl of gourmet slurps. But, reflecting its origins, the price for a bowl of ramen in Japan remains relatively low. Even shops that use only the highest quality ingredients rarely top ¥1000. The only problem with ramen is the lines at some of the better shops; an hour can be spent waiting for a bowl.

Types of ramen
Categorizing ramen can be tough. You can start with two basic types—heavy soups and clear soups. Heavy soups are created by cooking chicken and/or pork bones over high heat for many hours. The collagen is drawn out from the bones,

and the result is a creamy, heavy broth. Heavy soup varieties include tonkotsu ramen and miso ramen. Thinner soups, also made with pork and/or chicken bones, are cooked for a shorter time, but must be carefully tended to achieve a good flavor. These clear soups are mixed with either a soy sauce flavoring or a salt flavoring to create shoyu and shio ramen, respectively.

Of course, these four styles are only the beginning. Ramen is big on regionality, and a Tokyo-style shoyu ramen will differ from a Kitakata-syle shoyu ramen, which will be quite different from an Asahikawa-style shoyu ramen. A few regional favorites that pop up around the country are:

- Sapporo-style miso ramen. Yellow, wavy noodles in a thick miso soup topped with a layer of oil to keep the heat in.
- Kitakata-style shoyu ramen. Flattened noodles in a simple

shoyu broth, flavored with niboshi (dried anchovies). Eaten locally for breakfast.
- Saitama-style junk ramen. A soupless bowl, junk style, is filled with thick noodles topped with any ingredients that are fatty, salty, and full of flavor. A bowl might have chashu, pork back fat, spicy shrimp mayonnaise, cracker bits, a half-cooked egg, and a pile of cheese. Similar styles are also referred to as "abura-soba" (lit., "oil noodles") and "maze-men" ("mixed noodles").
- Tokyo-style tsukemen. Noodles served cold and dipped into a thick, hot soup. The soup is often pork based and mixed with different dried fish.
- Tokushima-style tonkotsu ramen. A thick, porky soup topped with a pork stir-fry and a raw egg.
- Hakata-style tonkotsu ramen. Often 100% pork, these bowls are heavy, stinky, and cheap. The noodles are as thin as possible, and served up al dente.

Using the ticket machine

Most ramen shops have a ticket machine near the door. Customers should buy a ticket before sitting down, and be ready to give their ticket to the staff when asked. Some ticket machines are daunting, with dozens of choices. In general, though, the upper left button on a ticket machine will get you a great bowl. When in doubt, go for the upper left.

Different styles of ramen are usually on different lines, with toppings and drinks at the bottom of the ticket machine. When in doubt, a simple request of "Sumimasen, osusume?" ("Excuse me, what do you recommend?") will get you some help if you need it.

Kaedama (extra noodles)

You can order this at some shops, especially tonkotsu ramen shops. When you finish your regular serving, but still have some soup left in the bowl, order kaedama. Simply say "Sumimasen" to get the staff's attention, then say "Kaedama onegai shimasu." You will probably be charged ¥100.

Vocabulary

rāmen ラーメン・らーめん・拉麺	ramen noodles
chūkasoba 中華そば	another name for ramen; lit., "Chinese noodles"
tsukemen つけ麺	noodles served separately and dipped into a stronger soup
shōyu 醤油	soy sauce
shio 塩	salt
tonkotsu 豚骨・とんこつ	literally "pork bone"; a thicker soup that is made with all or mostly pork bones
miso 味噌・みそ	fermented soy bean paste used to flavor a bowl of ramen

Toppings:

tokusei 特製	special (topping); this will typically include extra pork, an egg, and some other toppings of the shop's choosing
nori 海苔・のり	seaweed, laver
negi ネギ	green onions
moyashi もやし	bean sprouts
tamago たまご・卵	egg
chāshū チャーシュー	roasted slices of pork
kōn コーン	corn
batā バター	butter
menma メンマ	pickled bamboo shoots

Other menu items:

gyōza ぎょうざ・餃子	fried gyoza pork dumplings
biiru ビール	beer
kaedama 替玉	an extra order of noodles

Ramen in heavy soup

Muteppo (Ekoda)
無鉄砲

Thick tonkotsu ramen is nothing new. You'll find many shops all over the country serving bowls of it. But if you want the thickest, most intense bowl there is, Muteppo is the place to go. The soup is 100% pork bones, boiled for many, many hours. Just watching them stir the giant vats of soup is reason enough to come to this shop.

The tonkotsu ramen (¥780) is good, but do yourself a favor and get the chashumen (¥1030). It's covered with thinly sliced, tender pieces of pork that seem to melt into the soup. In typical tonkotsu fashion, you can specify the level of a few things in your bowl. If asked, just say "futsu," it will get you noodles cooked the regular way, the regular thickness of the soup, and a regular serving of green onions on top. If you finish your noodles and want some more, an order of kaedama (¥150) will get you what you want.

Located a bit north of Numabukuro station on the Seibu Shinjuku line.

Senrigan (Higashi-Kitazawa)
千里眼

There is a ramen shop in Japan called Jiro (not to be confused with the famous sushi shop of a similar name). Jiro features thick, wheaty noodles in a mega-porky soup. Add to that copious amounts of garlic, top with a mountain of bean sprouts, drizzle the whole thing with pork back fat, and you have the base of a bowl of Jiro ramen. There are other factors, but essentially this is a bowl that is tough to finish, and you'll smell like it for the next twelve hours.

Jiro has spawned many Jiro-style shops. One of the best is Senrigan. The soup is intense, but drinkable. The chashu is thick-cut, but tender. The toppings are plentiful, with raw garlic, back fat, spicy crisped rice, and the standard bean sprout pile all coming into play. Don't go for anything more than the normal ramen (¥730) here. Larger sizes of noodles or bowls with more pork are on the menu, but should only be attempted by a seasoned Jiro fan.

It should be noted that at any Jiro-style shop, you will be asked "Ninniku iremasu ka?" Basically, "You want garlic in that?" This is code for you to tell them how much of each topping you want. Many shops will get upset if you don't have an answer, so just remember to say "futsu." This will get you regular amounts of all the toppings, the best choice for a first timer.

Nagi Golden Gai (Shinjuku)
凪 ゴールデン街

Dried baby sardines (niboshi) have been a common ingredient in ramen for many years. It wasn't until recently, though, that ramen chefs began using them in abundance. The tiny fish have a very bitter flavor, and cooking them too long will ruin anything. So when a shop comes along that is able to extract as much smoky, fishy taste from their niboshi as possible, fans rejoice.

Golden Gai, in Shinjuku's Kabukicho entertainment district, is a sight to behold. With more bars per square meter than anywhere else in the world, you wouldn't expect an amazing ramen shop. But there it is, up on the second floor. Just look for the ever-present line. Feel free to drink before coming here, niboshi ramen is an amazing hangover preventative measure.

The menu is simple—go for either the niboshi ramen (¥820) or the niboshi ramen with egg (¥920). Squeeze in with the other happy slurpers, and enjoy some of the strongest soup in Tokyo. The noodles are rough as well, curly flat noodles that soak up just the right amount of the soup.

Kagari (Ginza)
篝 (Kagari)

Ginza is known for high-end fine dining. Half of the most expensive sushi restaurants in the world are there, as is a tempura shop that costs as much as a round trip ticket to Japan. It would make sense that ramen masters wouldn't consider trying to make a succesful ramen shop in the area. But when Kagari opened in 2013, word quickly spread. Ginza had a gourmet ramen shop that had normal ramen shop prices.

Be prepared to wait. The line on this back-alley shop usually requires at least thirty minutes. But once you are inside, you can really relax in this beautiful shop. Clean wooden fittings and staff dressed in sharp white jackets are a welcome respite. Order either the creamy chicken paitan (Paitan Yu Soba ¥950) or the robust niboshi ramen (niboshi shoyu soba ¥900). The first is made with chicken bones cooked over high heat for many hours, releasing the collagen in the bones. For people who like more of a rich soy sauce flavor, the niboshi ramen is the way to go.

The toppings are also worth mentioning at Kagari. The seasonal vegetables (kisetsu no yasai ¥380) match the chicken paitan quite well, adding splashes of color to the white soup. For the niboshi ramen, mushrooms from Kyoto (Kyotosan Takenoko ¥250) or roast Japanese beef (Kokusan Gyu-rosu biifu ¥400) are a must.

JAC (Koenji)
中華そばJAC

Tokushima, a major city on Japan's smallest major island of Shikoku, is home to one of the most famous local styles of ramen. The signature points are a heavy, porky soup flavored with soy sauce and topped with a sliced pork stir fry and a raw egg. A few shops have made the 600 km journey from Tokushima to Tokyo, and JAC is one of them.

JAC is actually more of a Tokushima-inspired bowl. Sure, the fried pork and raw egg are there, but the soup is a little more refined, blending chicken and pork to give a more mellow taste.

Their deluxe bowl (JAC Soba ¥900) is worth it; a bit more fried pork and an extra half-cooked egg make for a satisfying slurp.

KAKU-A (Yoyogi)
角栄

Miso ramen is prevalent in Japan, but few shops truly excel. It is an easy dish to make; season a thick soup with some miso paste and be done. But to make a memorable bowl, a ramen chef needs to blend the right amount of miso into the right soup, and pair it with the right noodles and toppings. Japan has dozens of local styles of miso, so this can be quite a task. Kaku-a uses miso from Niigata, known as Echigo miso. The master blends five different misos from the region to create his thick miso ramen. The menu is rather small, with a miso ramen and a curry miso ramen. Go for the regular miso (¥800) and top it with whatever looks good; cheese and an egg are popular.

Shinasoba Tanaka (Otsuka)
志奈そば 田なか

The master at Tanaka commutes in to this shop every day from the far side of Chiba, about two hours away. He is a surfer, and that part of Japan has some nice waves in the morning. That part of Japan is also famous for seafood, and the bowl at Tanaka reflects this.

Go for the Aji Nibo Soba (¥750). Aji, horse mackerel, and niboshi (dried sardines) are combined with plenty of Japanese konbu seaweed to make a thick, umami-rich bowl that has garnered a lot of attention since the shop opened in 2013.

Tuesdays, Wednesdays, and Fridays have special menu items that are worth checking out. A spicy bowl on Tuesday, a wine-steamed clam bowl on Wednesday, and a meatier version of their normal bowl on Friday.

Kikanbō (Kanda)
鬼金棒

You'll find spicy ramen on many shop's menus. This usually means they take their normal bowl, throw in some chili peppers, and call it a day. Many of these bowls are just hot, with very little in terms of complexity. Only a few shops really focus on balancing spice with other flavors to create an amazing bowl of ramen. Kikanbo goes beyond the call of duty with their spicy miso ramen.

The bowl of karashibi ramen (¥800) comes with two choices: how much hot spice, and how much numbing spice. The shop's hot spice should be approached with caution. Made with a blend of spices from around the world, the regular level is probably the best to start with. Higher levels should only be attempted by true spice fans. Kikanbo is heavy on the sansho, Chinese numbing peppercorn. This second spice blend is bitter and numbing. For first timers, when asked about the spice intensity they prefer, a simple futsu futsu—regular for both—is a good idea.

All that spice sits atop a miso soup, blended with house-made sansho oil and a heavy soup. Fans of stewed pork might consider getting the extra pork topping (¥200) for a large slab of stewed pork belly that melts into the bowl.

La-show-han (Ogawamachi)
担々麺本舗 辣椒漢

Tantanmen is a direct descendant of Chinese dandanmein. This dish of Sichuan origin is spicy, and a traditional bowl will have plenty of chili oil, Sichuan peppercorn, and minced pork. You can find tantanmen at many Chinese restaurants in Japan, but for the best bowls, you have to go to shops that specialize in the dish.

La-show-han is one of those shops. They serve nothing but tantanmen, though they have a few varieties. The Masamune Tantanmen (¥850) is a classic soupless style, but for fans of the bitter-hot Sichuan peppercorn, go for the Premium Masamune Tantanmen

(¥1000). It is full of spice, peppers, and flavored oils, though a bit of an overload for the uninitiated.

If you want tantanmen with soup, they offer a few varieties. The menu is easy to understand, with plenty of photos of the bowls.

Ramen in light soup

Yamaguchi (Takadanobaba)
らぁ麺 やまぐち

Takadanobaba is considered a bit of a ramen battle zone. Through the years, many shops have opened and closed, and to have a successful shop in this part of Tokyo is considered a great feat. Yamaguchi is probably the most famous new shop in the area.

Yamaguchi's ramen is, apart from a single slice of chashu on top, an entirely pork-free bowl of ramen. But this is no ordinary chicken soup. The shoyu flavoring is intense at first, with a smooth aftertaste. Go for the bowl with an egg (¥880), as the shop uses only the finest chickens from Iwate Prefecture. Matched with aged soy sauce and noodles from Kyoto, this is one that has a lot of thought put into it.

For those who want a pork-free bowl, make sure you tell them so. A simple "buta nashi" will suffice, and you'll probably get an extra slice of their amazing chicken chashu instead of the pork.

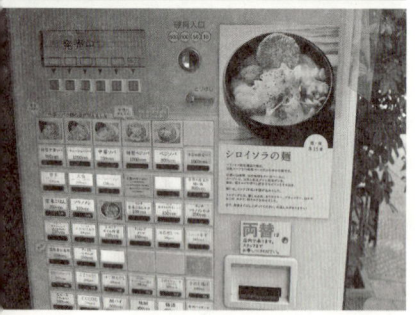

Soranoiro (Kojimachi)
ソラノイロ

Ramen is often thought of as a manly food in Japan. Dirty shops with an air thick with oil fumes would have most pretty ladies heading to the local cafe for lunch instead. In recent years, a few chefs have designed not only their ramen, but their shops as well around the concept of accessibility and appeal for everyone. When Soranoiro opened it was immediately embraced by both men and women for its healthier options and its light, airy atmosphere.

The ticket machine is very easy to use; the upper row is four giant pictures. For traditionalists, go with the special chukasoba (¥990), a simple shoyu bowl that goes above and beyond with their choice of ingredients. Free-range local chicken from Kumamoto and small-batch soy sauce from Nagano are a couple of the premium bits that give this ramen a clean, refreshing taste.

But the bowl that has really garnered attention is the special veggie soba (¥1000). The soup is a thick pottage of carrots, cabbage, onions, and other vegetables. The special version comes topped with even more vegetables and a perfectly cooked egg. A very healthy-feeling bowl. It is not, however, a vegetarian bowl (some of the tare seasoning has animal products).

They also have an outlet at the Tokyo Ramen Street in Tokyo Station.

Saikoro (Nakano)
さいころ

The north side of Nakano is famed for Nakano Broadway, a center of otaku culture and interesting traditional restaurants. But on the often ignored south side, there is a wonderful ramen shop worth a visit. Saikoro is part of the Jiraigen Syndicate, a noodle group that makes simple, honest Tokyo ramen in cool, stylish shops. Look for the shop with a DJ booth and hanging saikoro (dice) in the window.

The ticket machine here is huge, but head to the upper row and look for the one with the niku 肉 (¥730). Niku means meat, and you'll get a bowl topped with slices of perfectly roasted chashu pork. The soup is a lighter shoyu base hit with a bit of dried fish. Add to that handmade noodles (the noodle factory is upstairs), and you have one of the best simple bowls in Tokyo.

Konjiki Hototogisu (Hatagaya)
金色 不如帰

Hototogisu is a little hard to find. It's located in a suburb a few stations west of Shinjuku, down a local shopping street, and in a nondescript alleyway. They usually have a line, which is the only indication of anything existing there. But therein lies the beauty of ramen. Hototogisu could make a killing with a bigger shop in a busier part of town, but they choose to stay, despite the countless awards and accolades.

Hototogisu blends a clear, meaty soup with a soup made from Japanese clams. The flavors are full of umami, and very refreshing. But what gives them their edge is the excellent flavoring of the toppings. The shoyu ramen (¥800) and the shio ramen (¥850) are both excellent and quite different. Though they use the same base soup, the shoyu is accented with homemade porcini mushroom flakes and oil, while the shio ramen is paired with truffle oil. Both of these bowls have a deep earthy taste that has most patrons drinking every last drop.

On Sundays they're open only at lunchtime.

Kabochan (Komagome)
麺屋KABOちゃん

This tiny ramen shop down a small shopping street was a hand-me-down to the current owner. Kubokawa-san, whose nickname is Kabo-chan, was a well repected ramen hunter before he took over this ramen and kakigori shop. Yes, this is one of those ramen shops that serves Japanese-style shaved ice.

The Shimofuri chukasoba (¥750), named after the small shopping street, is a simple, hearty bowl of shoyu ramen. The previous shop's master was also known for his shoyu ramen, and the training and influence are shown. But in recent years, Kabochan has become quite famous for his spiced miso ramen (R15 Otona no Spicy Miso Chuka Soba ¥850). Spices that seem at home in Indian cooking are blended with a rich miso base.

Rock'anDo (Ikebukuro)
麺屋 六感堂

The first thing you'll notice at Rock'anDo is the color scheme. Green is everywhere, from the signage to the little green army men on a shelf. This should clue you in—you'll be eating green ramen. Rock'anDo's signature dish uses a "superfood" called euglenids, a kind of algae-like organism rich in vitamins A, C, and E.

You should go for broke with the yuzu- and mitsuba-topped bowl of green noodles (yuzu mitsuba green men ¥850). The mitsuba, known as Japanese parsley, gives even more vibrant green color to the bowl. The fresh zest of Japanese yuzu citrus has a fragrant quality that sits quite well with shio ramen. Wash it all down with a green-bottled Heineken.

Papapapa Pine (Nishi-Ogikubo)
パパパパパイン

At first, pineapple ramen sounds strange, maybe even downright awful. But imagine some other things that have been matched with pineapples. Pineapple and a sweet teriyaki sauce make a great burger topping. Pineapple glaze is amazing on ham and pork chops. And thousands of Hawaiian-style pizzas are ordered every day. Does it work with ramen? You bet.

Papapapa Pine's interior is decorated from top to bottom with pineapples. Go for the shoyu with all the toppings (¥920). You'll get extra pork, extra chopped pineapple, and an egg that has been marinated in, you guessed it, pineapple juice. The soup isn't too sweet, just enough to match the saltiness of the soy sauce.

Papapapa Pine also has occasional limited bowls that use other fruit. Figs, bananas, and strawberries have all made their way into bowls at Papapapa Pine.

Special noodles —tsukemen and abura soba

Fūunji (Nishi-Shinjuku)
風雲児

Tsukemen is everywhere in Tokyo. Expecially tonkotsu gyokai tsukemen. Pork and chicken bones are cooked on high heat for a long time to draw out as much creamy collagen as possible. Thickness is the key here. This soup is usually blended with a fishy soup made from dried Japanese fish. The result is like gravy, and the flavor is like nothing else in the world. Serve cold noodles on the side for dipping, and you have a very popular style of tsukemen.

There are many shops like this, and they tend to be universally good. One stands out though, and when you finally make it inside Fuunji, you'll see why it is considered a top spot for tsukemen in Tokyo. The line is always there, stretching out, across the street, and sometimes veering into the nearby park. The line moves fast, so jump in.

Be sure to order the tsukemen here (¥800). The ramen on the menu is good, but the tsukemen is where it's at. You'll be asked what size portion of noodles you want when you hand in your ticket. Nami gets you regular, and dai gets you a large size. Unless you are very hungry, go for the nami. Fuunji uses only chicken in their soup, something that is rarely done. Blended with a thick fish stock, and topped with fish powder, this one really clings to the noodles. The smoky, roasted taste can be enjoyed after the noodles are gone by diluting the soup with some broth, located on the counter.

Gachi (Akebonobashi)

Gachi

There's no better way to enjoy amazing, housemade ramen noodles than in a bowl of abura soba. Literally meaning oil-noodles, abura soba leaves the soup out, with only some tare seasoning, oils, and toppings. Gachi, part of the Mensho ramen group, has a noodle factory in the back. Depending on the time you go, you might see someone back there feeding sheets of dough through the noodle machine, prepping for the next day.

Go for the regular abura soba (¥690), or if you love chashu go for the chashu abura soba (¥890). An important note with abura soba, you need to mix it vigorously. Mix, mix, mix, then mix some more. All this mixing activates some of the gluten in the noodles, and will make it taste even better. Eat a bite or two, then add in a few squirts of hot oil and vinegar. Have a couple more bites, and then add in any of the shop's other free toppings. Crispy noodle bits, herb garlic, spicy mayo, and more. This is a fun, messy bowl that really satisfies.

Data

Muteppo (Ekoda)　　　　　　　　　03-5380-6886
無鉄砲
Egota 4-5-1, Nakano-ku
Open 11am-3, 6-11pm. Closed Mondays.

Senrigan (Higashi-Kitazawa)　　　03-3481-5773
千里眼
Komaba 4-6-8, Meguro-ku
Open 11am-2:30, 5-9:45pm daily.

Nagi Golden Gai (Shinjuku)　　　　03-3205-1925
凪 ゴールデン街
Kabukicho 1-1-10-2F, Shinjuku-ku
Open 24 hours a day.

Kagari (Ginza) — unlisted
篝 (Kagari)
Ginza 4-4-1, Chuo-ku
Open 11am-3:30, 5-10:30pm (Sat -9pm). Closed Sundays.

JAC (Koenji) — 03-5318-5240
中華そばJAC
Koenji-Kita 1-4-12, Suginami-ku
Open 11:30am-3, 6pm-midnight. Closed Sun eve, Mon.

KAKU-A (Yoyogi) — 03-3341-4100
角栄
Sendagaya 5-29-27, Shibuya-ku
Open 11am-11pm daily.

Shinasoba Tanaka (Otsuka) — 03-3988-0118
志奈そば 田なか
Higashi-Ikebukuro 2-19-2, Toshima-ku
Open 11am-3, 5-10pm (Sat 11-3). Closed Sundays.

Kikanbō (Kanda) — 03-3256-2960
鬼金棒
Kajicho 2-10-10, Chiyoda-ku
Open 11am-4, 5:30-9pm. Closed Sundays.

La-show-han (Ogawamachi) — 070-2181-0168
担々麺本舗 辣椒漢
Kanda Nishikicho 1-4-8, Chiyoda-ku
Open 11am-3pm (Sat -2pm), 5:30-8pm. Closed Sundays.

Yamaguchi (Takadanobaba) — 03-3204-5120
らぁ麺 やまぐち
Nishi-Waseda 2-11-13, Shinjuku-ku
Open 11:30am-3, 5:30-9pm (Sat, Sun 11:30-9). Closed Mondays.

Soranoiro (Kojimachi) — 03-3263-5460
ソラノイロ
Blue Bldg North 1B, Hirakawacho 1-3-10, Chiyoda-ku
Open 11am-3:30, 6-10pm (LO; Sat, Sun 11-5). Closed first Sunday.

Saikoro (Nakano) — 03-6304-8902
さいころ
Nakano 2-28-8, Nakano-ku
Open 11am-1:30am (LO; Sun -11pm) daily.

Konjiki Hototogisu (Hatagaya) — 03-3373-4508
金色 不如帰
Hatagaya 2-47-12, Shibuya-ku
Open 11:30am-3, 6:30-10pm. Closed Thu; Fri; Sun eve.

Kabochan (Komagome) — unlisted
麺屋KABOちゃん
Nishigahara 1-54-1, Kita-ku
Open 11:30am-3, 5:30-9pm. Closed Wednesdays.

Rock'anDo (Ikebukuro) — 03-5952-6006
麺屋 六感堂
Higashi-Ikebukuro 2-57-2, Toshima-ku
Open 11am-9pm daily.

Papapapa Pine (Nishi-Ogikubo) — 03-3247-2181
パパパパパイン
Nishiogi-Minami 3-12-1, Suginami-ku
Open 11am-11pm (Sun -8pm) daily.

Fūunji (Nishi-Shinjuku) — 03-6413-8480
風雲児
Yoyogi 2-14-3, Shibuya-ku
Open 11am-3, 5-9pm. Closed Sundays.

Gachi (Akebonobashi) — 03-6380-4874
Gachi
Sumiyoshicho 7-10, Shinjuku-ku
Open 11am-3, 5-10pm. Closed Sundays.

Chapter 3

International influences

日本流

Online Map
bento.com/maps/intl.html

Japanese curry

カレーライス

Surveys of Japanese schoolchildren reveal curry to be their very favorite dish, and affection for this ubiquitous comfort food extends into adulthood—along with ramen, curry rice is one of Japan's national dishes. Its presence on menus dates back to the 1870s when it first made its way to Japan via the British navy, which explains why it was originally a type of 'yoshoku,' or classic European cuisine. From early in its history, Japanese curry has had its own special character, very distinct from Indian, Thai, Vietnamese, Malaysian, or indeed British dishes of the same name.

    A few different styles are popular in Japan. "Ofuu" (European) curries are a mix of European and Indian influences—basically the roux incorporates Indian spices simmered in a European-style stew based on meat or chicken stock. "Indo" (Indian) style curries leave out the stock. A third category is "original" curries, which can be found on the menus of trendy modern cafes as well as dedicated restaurants. These are often inspired by Thai or other coconut-based curries, and can incorporate a wide variety of vegetables and other ingredients.

European-style curry restaurants can be especially quirky—the style saw a boom in popularity around forty or fifty years ago, and today original shops from that era can often be recognized by their French-sounding names and classic 1970s-era Japanese coffeeshop decor—heavy wooden tables, white stucco walls hung with paintings, artistic knickknacks scattered about, and bebop-era jazz playing in the background.

Generally these shops let you choose from a variety of base ingredients (meats and/or shellfish) and toppings (mushrooms, cheese, boiled quail eggs). Curries are ladled from a small gravy boat onto a plate of white rice that's dotted with bits of cheese. Boiled potatoes and colorful pickled condiments are served on the side.

Whatever the style of curry, you will usually be asked how spicy you want your dish. "Ama-kuchi" means not at all spicy, "kara-kuchi" means spicy, and "chu-kara" is somewhere in the middle. Sometimes there will be several levels of spiciness; in this case there's usually a numbered system listed on the menu, and you can choose your level by number.

Curries, especially European-style, can often be found in yoshoku restaurants. Udon served in a curry-flavored soup is another popular curry-based dish, and is covered starting on page 114.

Vocabulary

karē　カレー　curry

ōfū karē　欧風カレー　"European-style" curry

indofū karē　インド風カレー・印度風カレー　"Indian-style" curry

biifu　ビーフ　beef

pōku　ポーク　pork

chikin　チキン　chicken

ebi　えび・海老　shrimp, prawn

hotate　ホタテ・帆立　scallop

karasa　辛さ　level of spiciness

kara-kuchi　辛口　spicy

ama-kuchi　甘口　not spicy

chū-kara　中辛　medium-spicy

Yamituki (Takadanobaba)
ヤミツキカリー 早稲田店

Original recipes, unique flavors and ample use of fresh seasonal vegetables help Yamituki stand out in the highly competitive Japanese curry landscape. Umami-rich ingredients like ripe tomatoes, cheese and coconut milk add depth and bring out the individual flavors of the curries' vegetable and meat ingredients.

Some popular options (from ¥730) are oysters and spinach with baked cheese; ripe tomato, eggplant and chicken; and an outstanding pork-cabbage combo. Extra toppings (mostly ¥100) include corn, bamboo shoots, coriander, garlic shoots and tofu. Miniature blowtorches are used when preparing the curries with baked cheese.

Lunch is served until 4 pm. Yamituki has four other branches around town, with shops in Iidabashi, Nakano, and Jimbocho, and a small department-store counter in Ginza Printemps.

Tomato (Ogikubo)
トマト

This small neighborhood yoshoku-ya serves "European stews and English curries." Curry sauces are built on a fond de veau base and incorporate some 36 different spices, all on display on the shop's counter. The flavor of the curry is rather unique and very appealing—similar to other European-style Japanese curries but with an intriguing hint of medicinal herbs.

My personal favorite is the mild, "creamy" Hokkaido veal curry, especially with the optional seasonal vegetable add-on, which features ten different vegetables such as asparagus, okra and lotus root. There's also a popular beef-tongue curry, which might be an even better match for the rather assertive sauce. An order of veal curry with extra vegetables and dessert is priced at around ¥2000.

Moyan Curry (Nishi-Shinjuku)
もうやんカレー利瓶具（リビング）

With its exotic-ethnic decor and Hawaiian background music, the atmosphere here is closer to a Bohemian cafe than a curry shop. The curry menu itself is rather exotic too—variations include ratatouille, avocado, pig's foot, and leek curries. The "Zenbu" (everything) curry (¥1550) is a good introduction to Moyan's charms—it contains beef, pork, chicken, shrimp and cheese in a sweetish roux, and it's quite filling.

Besides the many curry variations you can also choose special toppings (grilled cheese, fried egg, mushrooms), adjust the size of your rice portion, and specify your desired degree of spiciness on a scale of zero to twenty. Pick from various salads and side dishes for a well-balanced meal; the Thai-style cucumbers with coriander (¥300) are one of my favorites. Drinks include simple cocktails, inexpensive wines (¥2000/bottle), Korean makkoli and beer.

Petit Feu a la Campagne (Hanzomon)
プティフ・ア・ラ・カンパーニュ

This off-the-beaten-track shop on a Hanzomon side street serves some of Tokyo's best European-style Japanese curries. The mixed curry with chicken, pork and beef is especially recommended—the meats are tender and skillfully prepared, the sauce rich and spicy. Curries come with a good-size helping of boiled potatoes. The coffee-shop decor is nicer than average, although it can get smoky when crowded.

Perusona (Jimbocho)
ペルソナ

Perusona serves top-quality European-style curries, and two- and three-ingredient combination curries are easy to order. The eggplant, chicken and beef combo (¥1400) is a standout here—the sauce is richly spiced and on the sweet side, while the beef is lean and very tender. The eggplant is a nice touch, adding some contrast to the ubiquitous meat ingredients. The spacious second-floor dining room is done up in classic 1970s coffeeshop style, with Brazilian easy-listening music and smooth jazz in the background.

Camp (Yoyogi)
野菜を食べるカレーcamp

The curries of this cult-favorite shop are known for their heavy use of vegetables, with variations such as four-bean keema, asparagus and bacon, and German potato and soft-boiled egg. The decor incorporates an outdoor camping theme, down to the camp-style cutlery and tableware. Lunch and dinner set menus average around ¥1000.

Bondy (Jimbocho)
ボンディ(Bondy)

Bondy's European-style curry sauce is scrumptious, with a natural fruit sweetness, well-balanced spices and complex flavors. There aren't many mixed-ingredient options, but the shrimp, clam and chicken combo is quite good. It features plump shrimps and juicy, flavorful clams along with button mushrooms, almonds and a sprig of watercress on top—a nice touch—plus umeboshi and a couple of sweet and delicious potatoes on the side.

The entrance is through a used bookstore—take the far right-hand aisle. Bondy gets extra points in my book for being open all afternoon. Prices average around ¥1500, and take-out is available.

Bon Appetit (Mita)
ボンナペティ

An old standby in the Mita neighborhood, this long-running basement shop has solid wooden furniture, stucco walls, odd little paintings and soft jazz playing in the background. The roux for the European-style curries is quite good, but what really sets this place apart is the quality of the meat— nice lean chunks of pork and very tasty and tender chicken. The mixed meat or all-chicken options are recommended. The boiled potatoes are also very nice.

Loup de Mer (Kanda)
神田ルー・ド・メール

Loup de Mer proves that good yoshoku cuisine needn't be stuck in a time warp. Hokkaido beef curry (¥1100) is accompanied by an appetizing salad of head cheese and red-cabbage slivers, plus soft but mildly crunchy deep-red pickles, with an enticing, almost cherry-like flavor. Hunks of beef are tender, lean and very flavorful, beautifully complemented by the curry sauce, rich but with a bracing tanginess.

The dining room is also very up to date, decorated in a tasteful pastel color scheme. Chef Suzuki is a veteran of the famous Dom Pierre yoshoku establishment, and his menu also covers yoshoku standards like hayashi rice and fried-rice omelettes.

Kitchen Nankai (Jimbocho)
キッチン南海

Addictive pork cutlet curry served with a dark, spicy sauce is the signature dish at this very old-fashioned, extremely down-to-earth counter shop. Curries start at around ¥580, and the very popular cutlet curry is ¥780.

Data

Yamituki (Takadanobaba) — 03-3205-0036
ヤミツキカリー 早稲田店
Nishi-Waseda 3-15-7, Shinjuku-ku
Open 11:30am-11:45pm daily.

Tomato (Ogikubo) — 03-3393-3262
トマト
Ogikubo 5-20-7, Suginami-ku
Open 11:30am-1:30, 5:30-9pm. Closed Tuesdays, 3rd Monday.

Moyan Curry (Nishi-Shinjuku) — 050-5787-1205
もうやんカレー利瓶具
Nishi-Shinjuku 6-25-14, Shinjuku-ku
Open 11:30am-2:30, 6-10:30pm (LO). Closed Sundays.

Petit Feu a la Campagne (Hanzomon) — 03-3234-4416
プティフ・ア・ラ・カンパーニュ
Ichibancho 8-13, Chiyoda-ku
Open 11:30am-9pm (LO). Closed Sundays.

Perusona (Jimbocho) — 03-3295-3578
ペルソナ
Matsumoto Bldg 2F, Kanda Jimbocho 1-28, Chiyoda-ku
Open 11:30am-3, 5:30-9pm (LO). Closed Sundays.

Camp (Yoyogi) — 03-5411-0070
野菜を食べるカレーcamp
Sendagaya 4-29-11, B1F, Shibuya-ku
Open 11:30am-10pm (LO). Closed Sundays.

Bondy (Jimbocho) — 03-3234-2080
ボンディ(Bondy)
Kosho Center 2F, Kanda Jimbocho 2-3, Chiyoda-ku
Open 11am-10pm daily.

Bon Appetit (Mita) — 03-3452-8062
ボンナペティ
Shiba 4-6-16, Minato-ku
Open 11am-3, 5:30-9:30pm. Closed weekends.

Loup de Mer (Kanda) 03-5298-4390
神田ルー・ド・メール
Uchi-Kanda 3-10-7, 2F, Chiyoda-ku
Open 11:30am-2:30, 5:30-8:30pm (LO; -6 Sun). Closed Mondays.

Kitchen Nankai (Jimbocho) 03-3292-0036
キッチン南海
Kanda Jimbocho 1-5, Chiyoda-ku
Open 11:15am-4, 4:45-8pm. Closed Sundays.

Yōshoku

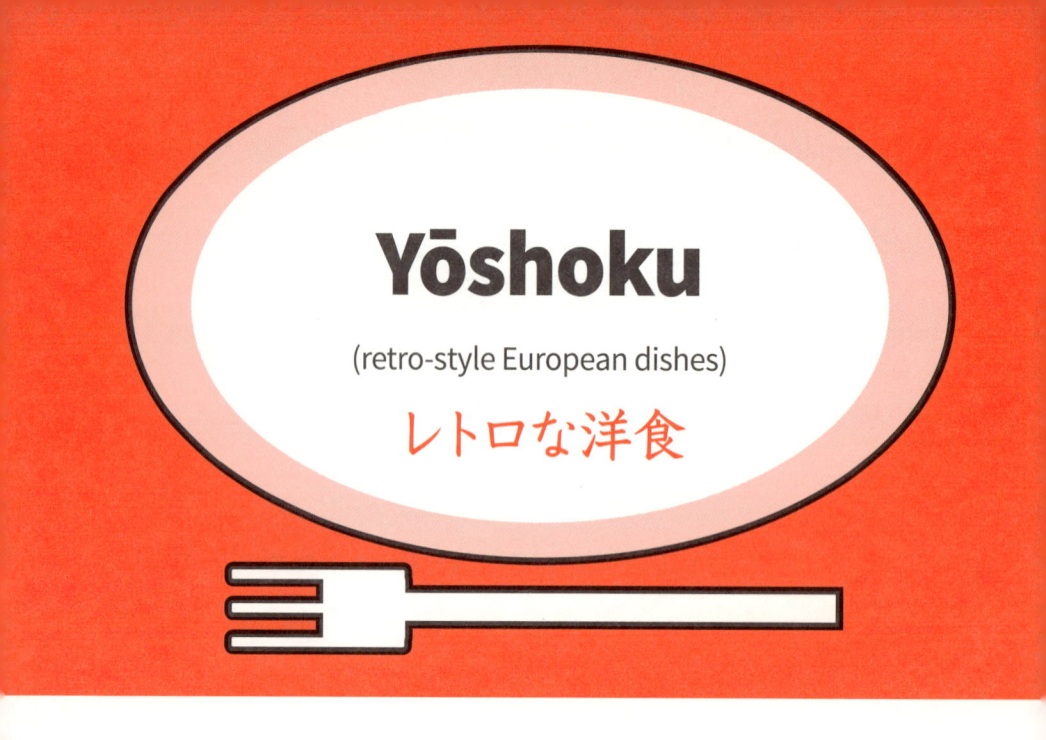

(retro-style European dishes)

レトロな洋食

While the word "yōshoku" literally just means "Western food," the term generally refers to a handful of classic dishes that were first introduced to Japan in the early twentieth century, when European culture was still quite exotic. With recipes and flavors adapted to long-ago Japanese tastes, yoshoku dishes have established themselves as a specialty cuisine in their own right, distinct from their European origins.

The most common dishes are fried-rice omelettes, ground-meat Hamburg steaks, stuffed cabbbage rolls, croquettes, beef stew with demi-glace, deep-fried prawns with tartar sauce, and "hayashi rice" (sliced beef and onions in gravy over white rice). Japanese curry rice and wafu spaghetti are also categories of yoshoku cuisine, covered in their own separate chapters.

Restaurants that specialize in yoshoku dishes appeal to

people's nostalgic feelings for a bygone era, and they often reflect a retro-chic aesthetic in their decor, sometimes intentionally. Even today, when world-class European restaurants thrive in cosmopolitan Tokyo, there's an unmistakable appeal in finding a beautiful rendition of a simple fried-rice omelette or cabbage roll or Hamburg steak, lovingly prepared in traditional, early twentieth-century style.

Vocabulary

hayashi raisu	ハヤシライス	sliced beef and onions in gravy (over rice)
hanbāgu	ハンバーグ	ground-meat Hamburg steak
rōru kyabetsu	ロールキャベツ	stuffed-cabbage rolls
korokke	コロッケ	croquettes
kani kuriimu korokke	かにクリームコロッケ	creamy crabmeat croquette
biifu shichū	ビーフシチュー	beef stew
ebi-furai	海老フライ	deep-fried prawns
omuraisu	オムライス	fried-rice omelette

Hamburg Will (Shinjuku Gyoen-mae)
ハンバーグ ウィル

The all-pork Hamburg steak here is made from premium Iwanaka pork from Iwate Prefecture, and it's remarkably tasty—a revelation in how good this simple dish can get. The ground meat is a mix of four different cuts of pork—shoulder, skirt steak, belly and cheek—resulting in an ideal balance of flavors and fat content. The patties are quite thick and ovaloid in shape, cooked to a juicy medium-rare consistency with slight grill-charring on the surface.

Steaks are served with a choice of sauce—demi-glace, yuzu-kosho or creamy mustard—but the meat is so moist and flavorful that the sauce seems superfluous. At lunchtime plain Hamburg steaks start at ¥1000, while variations such as mozzarella, pancetta and foie gras run a bit more. The mozzarella works quite well as a filling—the mild cheese enhances the flavor of the meat without competing with it.

Lunch comes with a nice cup of cabbage-tomato soup, and for an extra ¥380 the set menu includes salad and coffee or tea. The salad dressing incorporates various fruit juices, and the salad itself has bits of sausage hidden among the greens. Coffee comes with real cream. Other drink options include fruit juices, ginger-infused vinegar drink, and homemade fruit wines.

Limelight (Ichigaya)
らいむらいと

A Hamburg steak with cheese, in hefty sizes ranging from 200–300g, is one of the best selling dishes at this popular steakhouse. The ground steak is served with mashed potatoes and turnip, covered in chives and bits of toasted onion, and drenched in a very tasty garlic-butter sauce that really brings out the flavor of the meat.

The menu also features regular beef, chicken and pork steaks and roast beef as well as a few fried dishes and donburi items at lunchtime. The restaurant is spread out over two floors—the ground floor for smokers and the basement for non-smokers—and they do a lively lunchtime business. Hamburg steak with cheese starts at ¥1380 at lunchtime, ¥1728 at dinner. No dinner on Saturdays.

Vimon (Yaesu)
Vimon（ビモン）

The specialty here is Hamburg steak made from "Japanese black cattle," aka domestic Angus beef. The "sune burg" (ground shank steak) starts at ¥1430 for a reasonably hefty 170g portion, which at lunchtime comes with soup, salad and butter-infused garlic bread. It's served without any sauce and prepared with minimal filler, so that the flavor of the meat shines through, and indeed the patty is quite juicy, with optimal fat content. Lunch specials run until 5 pm.

Gooburg (Yotsuya 3-chome)
ぐーばーぐ

Gooburg presents a modern take on the Hamburg steak, producing both mixed-meat (pork and beef) and 100% beef versions. These are hefty and meaty, lightly browned on the surface but very tender in the middle—so tender that they're served with chopsticks rather than knife and fork. Each "hamburg" is served on a sizzling hot metal plate that arrives with a protective brown-paper wrapper to control splatter.

Variations include bacon and cheese toppings, Japanese grated daikon, and a version topped with ten different vegetables like cauliflower, kabocha pumpkin, bean sprouts and lotus root. There are also seasonal specials, such as the autumn hamburg served with enoki mushrooms in a porcini-mushroom-flavored sauce. Toasted garlic chips make a nice optional add-on.

Hamburg steaks start at around ¥700 a la carte, with side dishes like Caesar salad starting at around ¥400. Drinks include five or six inexpensive wines, whiskey, cocktails and soft drinks. The restaurant decor is evocative of a family restaurant, somewhat brightly lit, with bouncy pop music playing in the background.

Tsubame Kitchen (Marunouchi)
つばめキッチン

This venerable yoshoku specialist first opened in 1930, and they serve various types of Hamburg steak along with cabbage rolls and hayashi rice. This is modern yoshoku, though, so you can enjoy starters like Caesar salad, pate de campagne or marinated herring, while a variety of German wines—three by the glass and several more by the bottle—feature on the drinks list.

The Hamburg steak here is quite juicy and flavorful, like a fattier, more umami-rich version of meatloaf. One version is topped with beef stew instead of demi-glace sauce, offering an interesting contrast of beefy flavors; other variations come with a fried egg or with Japanese-style grated daikon and soy sauce. Sauteed chicken, salmon meuniere, pork pepper steak and homemade sausages round out the mains section of the menu.

The dining room is pleasantly decorated in modern retro style, with old posters and bold graphics, and there are plenty of two-tops and counter seats for lone diners. Budget ¥1800–3000 at dinnertime for food and drink.

Kurofunetei (Ueno)
黒船亭

This traditional shop offers all your yoshoku favorites—cabbage rolls with cheese, Hamburg steaks, seafood curry, fried-rice omelettes—but the big draw is their famous hayashi rice (¥1570). The beef is braised in a dark, umami-rich demi-glace sauce that's been simmered for a full week, lightly drizzled with cream and served over white rice. There's quite a bit of meat in each serving, all of it very tender. If you feel like splashing out, you can upgrade from regular beef to premium wagyu for a somewhat higher price.

The fried-rice omelettes are also nicely prepared, almost runny rather than fluffy, with a mushroomy fried-rice filling, and the crab croquettes are stuffed with big chunks of sweet crabmeat. If you want to try several popular items at the same time, the B Bento set (¥2980) includes Hamburg steak in mushroom sauce, beef tongue braised in red-wine sauce, a small omelette, crab or shrimp croquettes, soup, salad and rice.

Wines range from ¥1850–6480 per bottle, and there are evening set menus from around ¥5000. English-language menus are available.

Rengatei (Ginza)
煉瓦亭

Going strong since 1895, this Ginza fixture was the birthplace of not one but two yoshoku classics—hayashi rice and omu-rice (fried-rice omelette), and they still serve them the same way. The hayashi rice incorporates a decent-sized helping of beef in a hearty, slightly sweet sauce. It's ¥1600 at dinnertime, while omu-rice is ¥1400.

Nowadays the drinks list offers Guinness Stout, which matches the food quite well, and budget wines that are better than expected. The decor is charmingly dowdy, and the jazz soundtrack goes with the nostalgic mood. English menus are available.

Raifukutei (Ningyocho)
来福亭

Founded in 1904, this charming, tiny shop is famous for their hayashi rice, omelettes and katsudon. The hayashi rice (¥750) is quite straightforward: it's mostly sauce, thick, rich and beefy, with small bits of meat and onions floating in it, and it feels like it wouldn't be out of place in a school cafeteria. While it's not as fancy (or as meaty) as some of the other versions you'll find around town, it may come closest to the original form of the dish when it was invented back around the turn of the twentieth century.

The menu also offers more meat-centered options like sauteed pork and sauteed chicken, as well as curry rice and menchi katsu (deep-fried minced meat patties), all priced in the ¥750–1000 range.

Mantenboshi (Marunouchi)
グリル 満天星 丸ビル店

Mantenboshi serves a full range of updated yoshoku fare, including a fancy version of omu-rice—an omelette filled with fried rice that's flavored with ketchup, as the English-language menu helpfully explains. The fried-rice filling is dotted with bits of crunchy vegetables, sweet green peas and very flavorful mushrooms, while the omelette casing is topped with a savory brown sauce and big shrimps reminiscent of a Chinese stir-fry. It all adds up to a surprisingly exotic flavor combination—certainly not your run-of-the-mill omelette.

The omu-rice is ¥1150 at lunchtime, or you can get it as half of a "one plate mix" (¥2000), which also includes your choice of beef curry, fried prawn, stuffed cabbage, crab croquettes, seafood pilaf, Hamburg steak, or fried oysters in season. There are several other lunch specials, served all afternoon until 5 pm.

Tsutsui (Kayabacho)
津々井

Open since 1949, this old-school shop serves legendary fried-rice omelettes, Hamburg steaks, and many other standards. The chicken fried-rice omelette (¥1750 at dinnertime) is reasonably substantial, the flavorful rice filled with tasty chunks of chicken and mushrooms surrounded by a soft, almost runny layer of egg. There's a rather assertive ketchup-type tomato sauce for those who like that sort of thing, but I found it unnecessary.

They also do an unusual "torotoro" rice omelette (¥2000) where they mix the rice, egg and crabmeat filling together before cooking, then serve the rough-textured omelette with two contrasting types of tomato sauce. The dining room is old-fashioned in style and brightly lit, up on the second floor past the ground-floor open kitchen.

Azabu Shokudo (Nishi-Azabu)
麻布食堂

Omu-rice (fried-rice omelettes) and menchi katsu (deep-fried minced-meat cutlet) are the staples at this popular neighborhood establishment, along with Hamburg steaks and crab croquettes. The omelette is traditional in style, with a dark-hued fried-rice filling that's flavored with a mixture of ketchup and tomato sauce, and studded with bits of chicken and onion. The egg is just barely set, and it's served with your choice of three dressings—plain ketchup, demi-glace sauce or white sauce.

The basement dining room is spacious and comfortable, if a bit old-fashioned, with an outdoor sunken patio at one end. Omelettes, menchi-katsu and hayashi rice start at ¥980 at lunchtime, and ¥1200 in the evening. At night there's a small wine list starting at ¥3000 per bottle. Take-out is available.

Data

Hamburg Will (Shinjuku Gyoen-mae) — 03-3358-4161
ハンバーグ ウィル
YKB Shinjuku Gyoen Bldg 1F, Shinjuku 1-3-8, Shinjuku-ku
Open 11:30am-2, 5:30-8pm (LO) daily.

Limelight (Ichigaya) — 03-3230-2593
らいむらいと
Paddy Homes Hitokuchizaka B1F/1F, Kudan-Minami 3-4-8, Chiyoda-ku
Open 11am-2, 5:30-9pm (LO). Closed Sundays, holidays.

Vimon (Yaesu) — 03-3283-1841
Vimon
Kitchen Street (1F), Marunouchi 1-9-1, Chiyoda-ku
Open 11am-10pm (LO) daily.

Gooburg (Yotsuya 3-chome) — 03-3225-5675
ぐーばーぐ

Sano Bldg 1F, Yotsuya 3-7, Shinjuku-ku

Open 11am-10:30pm (LO) daily.

Tsubame Kitchen (Marunouchi) — 03-5252-7900
つばめキッチン

Marunouchi Oazo 5F, Marunouchi 1-6-4, Chiyoda-ku

Open 11am-11pm (LO; Sat, Sun 4pm-) daily.

Kurofunetei (Ueno) — 03-3837-1617
黒船亭

Kikuya Bldg 4F, Ueno 2-13-13, Taito-ku

Open 11:30am-10pm (LO) daily.

Rengatei (Ginza) — 03-3561-3882
煉瓦亭

Ginza 3-5-16, Chuo-ku

Open 11:15am-2:15, 4:40-8:30pm (LO). Closed Sundays.

Raifukutei (Ningyocho) — 03-3666-3895
来福亭

Nihonbashi Ningyocho 1-17-10, Chuo-ku

Open 11:30am-2, 5-9pm. Closed weekends.

Mantenboshi (Marunouchi) — 03-5288-7070
グリル 満天星 丸ビル店

Marunouchi Bldg. 5F, Marunouchi 2-4-1, Chiyoda-ku

Open 11am-10:30pm daily.

Tsutsui (Kayabacho) — 03-3551-4759
津々井

Shinkawa 1-7-11, Chuo-ku

Open 11am-1:30, 5-9pm (LO). Closed Sundays.

Azabu Shokudo (Nishi-Azabu) — 03-3409-4767
麻布食堂

Azabu West B1F, Nishi-Azabu 4-18-1, Minato-ku

Open 11:30am-2, 5:30-9:30pm (LO). Closed Sundays, Mondays.

Wafū spaghetti

(Japanese-style)

和風スパゲティー

Many decades ago, long before Italian restaurants occupied every neighborhood in Tokyo, there were simple Japanese spaghetti shops. These restaurants served, and still serve, not only tomato- and cream-based Italian pastas but also Japanese-style bowls incorporating ingredients like spicy cod roe, shimeji mushrooms, squid, sea urchin, and shiso leaves, often flavored with soy sauce. Toasted nori (seaweed) frequently appears as a topping, and aonori powder (an aromatic dried green seaweed) is a popular condiment.

You can still find a handful of these original shops around town, along with newcomers that offer contemporary Italian starters and side dishes to complement their Japanese pastas. In addition to offering unique flavors, one appealing aspect of many of these shops is their wide choice of ingredients and toppings, allowing diners to endlessly fine-tune their bowls.

Wafū spaghetti

Chapter 3 International influences

Vocabulary

supagetti	スパゲッティ	spaghetti
wafū	和風	Japanese-style
mentaiko	明太子	spicy salted cod (or pollock) roe
tarako	たらこ	salted cod (or pollock) roe
asari	あさり	short-neck clams
ika	いか	squid
ikura	いくら	salmon roe
kinoko	きのこ	kinoko mushrooms
nattō	納豆	sticky fermented soybeans

Pasta Kitchen (Nakano)
パスタ キッチン

Open since 1999, this pleasantly decorated basement shop serves several dozen variations of Japanese-style spaghetti—permutations of ingredients like tarako (cod roe), mentaiko (spicy cod roe), sea urchin, squid, natto, shiso, kimchee, shimeji and other mushrooms, eggplant and bacon.

The tarako, sea urchin, squid and shiso pasta (¥1180) is a nice mix of fresh flavors and contrasting textures, and it's a safe choice if you can't decide, or if you can't make it all the way through the voluminous Japanese menu. The noodles are served al dente, and crushed red peppers and aonori are provided for seasoning.

Other options include a dozen Japanese-style "soup spagetti" dishes (noodles served in a bowl of soupy sauce), as well as more standard Italian-style tomato, cream, meat and garlic-based sauces. Pasta bowls come in four different sizes, with between 100 and 200 grams of spaghetti.

The dimly lit dining room is nicer than average for this type of cuisine, with paintings on the walls and soft jazz playing in the background. Budget around ¥1000–1500 for pasta; there are also salads and other side dishes if you want a more balanced meal.

Spajiro (Akasaka)
すぱじろう 赤坂店

One of the draws of this retro-style Japanese spaghetti chain is the ability to customize your bowl almost endlessly. Spaghetti comes in tomato-based, cream-based and Japanese-style (soy sauce-flavored) sauces, with more than fifty variations in basic ingredients, twenty-five optional toppings, and four different portion sizes. To make things simpler for confused diners, the menu features a top-ten list.

The Japanese pasta section features ingredients like tarako and mentaiko (cod or pollock roe), asari clams, ikura (salmon roe) and natto (sticky fermented soybeans) in various combinations. Nicely toasted garlic chips are a recommended topping, and condiments include bottles of red-pepper oil rather than the usual Tabasco.

Spajiro has a more modern take on Japanese pasta than other restaurants of this genre—the decor is up to date, and side dishes include appealing items like arancini rice balls, bocconcini-tomato caprese; and spinach and kinoko mushrooms sauteed in garlic. Pastas start at under ¥1000, and side dishes and drinks are also reasonably priced.

Spajiro also has seven other branches in central Tokyo.

Hashiya (Yoyogi Koen)
ハシヤ 代々木八幡本店

This Japanese-spaghetti pioneer has been offering their unique take on pasta since the 1950s, with over sixty varieties on the menu. One of the more popular options features sea urchin, squid and cod roe, served in a sweet, buttery sauce flavored with soy sauce and topped with strips of nori seaweed.

Another crowd favorite is the shrimp and kinoko mushroom spaghetti, with big, flavorful shrimp in a sweet-tasting buttery sauce. They also offer a big selection of asari clam pastas served with an optional garlic sauce, and a dozen or so cod-roe variations. The noodles are pleasantly firm and chewy, and overall the flavors are well-balanced without being overpowering.

The old-fashioned dining room consists of a few tables plus a big counter area wrapping around the open kitchen. Budget around ¥1200–1500 for most pastas. On Wednesdays they serve lunch only, and close at 3 pm.

Hashiya (Nishi-Shinjuku)
ハシヤ 新宿店

A somewhat more accessible branch of Hashiya in Yoyogi Koen (see above), they serve the same huge selection of Japanese- and Italian-style spaghetti in an old-fashioned dining room in the basement of an office building.

Japonais (Ginza)
ジャポネ

The spartan lunch-counter decor looks like it hasn't been updated since the 1960s, and the food is similarly retro—Japanese-style spaghetti served with plastic tubs of potato salad as a side order. The mentaiko spaghetti is a heap of thick, soft-cooked pasta livened up with shiso leaves, shiitake, onions, nori and komatsuna greens nicely balancing the spicy cod roe.

Other options include the Jalico (shrimp and meat), Ume Nori (with a plum-flavored topping), China (featuring zasai pickles), and Kimchi (with pork). Regular portions are reasonably sized, and the jumbo size (for an extra ¥150) is almost comically large. Giant bottles of Tabasco and bowls of parmesan cheese are provided on the counter.

Pastas start at ¥500–600, and side salads are ¥100–150. The counter seats only thirteen people, but the line moves quickly. Open until 4 pm on Saturdays.

Al Dente (Nishi-Shinjuku)
あるでん亭 新宿店

While most of the spaghetti here at this old-fashioned pasta joint is served with tomato- or cream-based sauces, they also offer a nice Japanese-style mentaiko (spicy cod roe) spaghetti, with strips of nori seaweed and optional shrimp and/or squid. Pastas range from ¥1000–2000 depending on size and toppings.

Al Dente (Ginza)
あるでん亭 ソニービル店

Located high up in the Sony Building, this branch of Al Dente (see above) offers a nice view of Ginza's main drag to go with your noodles. Choose from some three dozen types of spaghetti, including Japanese-style variations like mentaiko (spicy cod roe). Cash only.

Data

Pasta Kitchen (Nakano) — 03-5340-3227
パスタ キッチン
Noi Bldg B1F, Nakano 2-25-6, Nakano-ku
Open 11:30am-3, 5-10:30pm (LO) daily.

Spajiro (Akasaka) — 03-3584-5550
すぱじろう 赤坂
Akasaka 3-15-9, Minato-ku
Open 11:30am-11pm daily.

Hashiya (Yoyogi-Koen) — 03-3466-1576
ハシヤ 代々木八幡本店
Tomigaya 1-3-10, Shibuya-ku
Open 11:30am-9pm (LO). Closed Thursdays.

Hashiya (Nishi-Shinjuku) — 03-3346-2371
ハシヤ 新宿店
Shinjuku Nomura Bldg. B2F, Nishi-Shinjuku 1-26-2, Shinjuku-ku
Open 11am-9pm. Closed Sundays.

Japonais (Ginza) — 03-3567-4749
ジャポネ
Ginza Inz #3, 1F, Ginza 2-2, Chuo-ku
Open 10:30am-8pm. Closed Sundays.

Al Dente (Nishi-Shinjuku) — 03-3349-0384
あるでん亭 新宿店
Shinjuku Center Bldg. BMF, Nishi-Shinjuku 1-25-1, Shinjuku-ku
Open 11am-9pm (LO; Sun -7:30pm) daily.

Al Dente (Ginza) — 03-3574-7470
あるでん亭 ソニービル店
Sony Bldg. 6F, Ginza 5-3-1, Chuo-ku
Open 11am-8pm (LO) daily.

Burgers

ハンバーガー

Tokyo has a good number of excellent gourmet burger joints, run by chefs who have studied and mastered the art of burger-making, and in fact entire books and websites have been devoted to reviewing and comparing the best burgers in town.

The best shops are known for the high quality of their ingredients, especially the meat used in the patty and the bacon and cheese toppings. Creative combinations of ingredients and dressings are a bonus, and of course tasty french fries and onion rings are always welcome.

Tokyo's gourmet burger shops usually offer a range of salads and other side dishes, beer and cocktails as well as soft drinks, and often milk shakes and American-style desserts. English-bilingual menus are quite common, and most burger shops do take-out, and often deliver within the immediate neighborhood.

Burgers

Vocabulary

bāgā　バーガー　burger

hanbāgā　ハンバーガー　hamburger

chiizu　チーズ　cheese

bēkon　ベーコン　bacon

wagyū　和牛　domestic Japanese beef

chiri　チリ　chili

daburu　ダブル　double (patty)

bābekyū　バーベキュー　barbecue (sauce)

furaido poteto　フライドポテト　French fries

onion ringu　オニオンリング　onion rings

abokado　アボカド　avocado

tēkuauto　テークアウト　take-out

Chapter 3 International influences

179

E·A·T (Gaienmae)
E·A·T（イーエーティー）

This ambitious American-style diner serves one of the few lamb burgers in town, and they do a terrific job (¥1300, or ¥1700 for a double patty). With minimal dressing on the burger, it's all about the very flavorful meat, beautifully grilled and lightly seasoned. If you prefer something beefier, the shop's flagship Kobe beef burger is very impressive, as are the regular wagyu burger and the Balentien burger, which is a spicy Cajun chicken patty.

The large menu is surprisingly diverse, with Tex Mex-style dishes (burritos, tacos, chili), spicy fare (Cajun roast chicken, jumbo shrimp with chile salsa), classic diner sandwiches (club house, NY steak), salads and soups. Most wines are priced ¥2400–6000 per bottle or ¥600 per glass, or you can opt for frozen margaritas or other cocktails. There's an English-language menu and take-out service. Budget around ¥3000 for dinner with drinks, ¥1200 for lunch.

Blacows (Ebisu)
ブラッカウズ

Run by a Japanese meat company, Blacows specializes in gourmet burgers made from black Angus wagyu beef, coarsely ground and very juicy. A full-time butcher occupies one corner of the kitchen and prepares all the meat for the patties.

The signature dish here is the bacon cheese avocado burger; it uses colby and monterey jack cheeses, original tartar sauce and tomato-vegetable barbecue sauce, marinated onion cubes, and bacon made from premium Nadeshiko Pork. Buns are produced in collaboration with the Maison Kayser bakery.

Plain burgers start at ¥1200, and the side-dish menu is more ambitious than most—wagyu meatballs with four cheeses, lobster bisque, voluminous Cobb salads. Wines are ¥3800–4000 per bottle or ¥750 per glass. Service is generally attentive, and the decor is tasteful. Take-out service is available.

Munch's Burger Shack (Mita)
マンチズバーガー シャック

Smoked bacon and a wide selection of cheeses (cheddar, gouda, colby, mozzarella and pepper jack) liven up the 100% US beef burgers here, along with American-style toppings like avocado, chili beans and mushrooms. Onion rings are crisp and tasty; other side options include fried chicken and an avocado-bacon Caesar salad.

Milk shakes come in exotic flavors—caramel, espresso, honey nuts—as well as your standard vanilla, chocolate and strawberry. A plain single burger with no toppings is ¥1080, while a double cheeseburger is ¥1800. Saturday hours are 11:30 am–8:30 pm, and Sundays they're open 11:30 am–6:30 pm. Delivery is available locally.

Cafe Hohokam (Harajuku)
Cafe Hohokam（ホホカム）

Choose from more than two dozen burger variations at this comfortable American-style cafe, including fun combinations like baked apple and gorgonzola, or chili, cheddar and jalapeno. They also offer a dozen different sandwiches, including a decent grilled-cheese that combines cheddar and mozzarella.

Burgers and sandwiches come with fries, and at lunchtime (11:30 am–4 pm) you also get a baby leaf salad and a coffee or other soft drink. There are nine different wines starting at ¥2600/bottle, and a good selection of US craft beers by the bottle.

The large outdoor terrace, furnished with a wooden deck, rattan furniture and lots of cactus plants, is quite popular when the weather is good.

Fatz's (Koenji)
Fatz's（ファッツ）

Run by an experienced American burger chef, this friendly neighborhood shop custom-assembles all its hamburgers according to your instructions. A basic, single 120-gram beef patty on a bun with cole slaw and fries runs ¥800—after that you can add on various toppings (provolone, fresh salsa, guacamole, jalapenos) and sauces (basil mayo, spicy ketchup) for a bit extra. You can also swap in chicken or sausage instead of the beef patty, or get a double-sized patty.

While you're waiting for your burger, the nachos con carne (¥850) are a great side dish—tortilla chips covered with two types of melted cheese, fresh salsa, guacamole, and some great chili. Fudge-brownie sundaes are available for dessert, and milkshakes come in a "cookies and cream" flavor as well as chocolate, vanilla and strawberry.

Drinks options include imported US beers from Kona, Anchor, and Brooklyn breweries as well as California wines and Mojitos. In addition to counter seating there's one picnic table out front in the courtyard. Everything on the menu is available to take out.

Fire House (Hongo)
Fire House

A pioneer of Tokyo's gourmet hamburger scene, this charmingly rustic little shop offers more than a dozen burgers to choose from, with variations like apple-mozzarella, mushroom-mozzarella and coriander-avocado-tomato guacamole. The hamburger meat is juicy, bacon (when you order it) is properly crisp, and relish and other condiments are restrained.

Burgers start at ¥1069, and come with a side order of fries; other sides include deep-fried octopus, fried mozzarella and onion rings.

Data

E·A·T (Gaienmae) — 03-6459-2432
E·A·T
Minami-Aoyama 2-27-18, Minato-ku
Open 11:30am-5:30, 6-10pm (LO) daily.

Blacows (Ebisu) — 03-3477-2914
ブラッカウズ
Ebisu-Nishi 2-11-9, Shibuya-ku
Open 11am-11pm daily.

Munch's Burger Shack (Mita) — 03-6435-3166
マンチズバーガー シャック
i-smart Bldg 1/2F, Shiba 2-26-1, Minato-ku
Open 11:30am-2:30, 5:30-8:30pm (LO). Closed Mondays.

Cafe Hohokam (Harajuku) — 03-5775-5708
Cafe Hohokam
Jingumae 3-22-14, 2F, Shibuya-ku
Open 11:30am-10:30pm (LO) daily.

Fatz's (Koenji) — 03-6762-3939
Fatz's
Lions Plaza Koenji E, Koenji-Kita 3-21-19, Suginami-ku
Open noon-3, 6-10pm (Sun noon-6pm). Closed Mondays, 3rd Tuesday.

Fire House (Hongo) — 03-3815-6044
Fire House
Hongo 4-5-10, Bunkyo-ku
Open 11am-10pm (LO; Sun. 7pm) daily.

Exotic sandwiches
サンドイッチの ニューウエーブ

Japan isn't the only place in the world with down-home "B-kyu" cuisines, and since Tokyo is a cosmopolitan and international city, adventurous diners here can explore some of the comfort foods of other lands. In this section I'd like to introduce a few sandwich shops, and sandwiches, that represent the ideals of B-kyu cuisines in their native countries.

First off, **banh mi** sandwiches are a popular local delicacy from Vietnam. With freshly baked French bread or rolls as the base, they showcase meaty fillings like roast pork, liver paste and ham, livened up with crunchy pickles and fresh cilantro leaves. In addition to the two shops listed here, you can sometimes find these sandwiches at regular Vietnamese restaurants.

Pinchos are open-faced Spanish-style sandwiches topped with everything from cold meats and seafood to stewed vegetables. I will introduce one budget-friendly pinchos specialist in Akasaka, but you can also find them in informal Spanish bars around town.

Lobster rolls have long been a popular snack in Maine, on the east coast of the US, and they've recently made inroads in New York and other urban areas. They're quite simply made, with seasoned lobster meat stuffed into a toasted, buttered bun. Two popular New York-based shops have brought their versions of this dish to the Tokyo area. Rounding out this section are noteworthy sandwiches from the Middle East, Argentina, and the Basque region along the French-Spanish border.

Vocabulary

sando(itchi) サンド（イッチ） sandwich

bainmii バインミー Vietnamese banh mi sandwich

hamu ハム ham

buta(niku) 豚(肉) pork

rebā pēsuto レバーペースト liver paste

chikin チキン chicken

pinchosu ピンチョス Spanish pinchos sandwich

robusutā rōru ロブスターロール lobster roll

Banh Mi Sandwich (Takadanobaba)
バインミーサンドイッチ

This simply named shop sells freshly made Vietnamese banh mi sandwiches in several enticing varieties, including roast pork, grilled chicken with honey and lemongrass, ham and liver paste, and shrimp avocado, all served on fresh-baked bread with crunchy, not-too-sour pickled vegetables.

Sandwiches are ¥500 each, and you can spring for extra coriander, liver paste, etc. for a little more. They also sell fresh-baked rolls in various flavors for ¥130. There's a tiny open-air seating area out front, but most customers are here for take-out.

Cafe Hai (Kiyosumi-Shirakawa)
カフェ ハイ

This arty little Vietnamese cafe turns out tasty fried-pork banh mi sandwiches that strike a nice flavor and texture balance between fatty, juicy pork, crunchy pickles, copious amounts of cilantro and lemongrass. They come with sides of shrimp chips and vegetable-tuna salad for ¥1000.

The rest of the pork-heavy menu

features down-home dishes like pho noodles with pork cakes, spring rolls, and "Com Tron Rau Thit"—steamed rice with ground pork and fresh vegetables. The cafe is located inside the Musuem of Contemporary Art Tokyo (MOT) building, just upstairs from the museum shop. They're closed for dinner but open all afternoon.

Lizarran (Akasaka)
リザラン

Budget pinchos snacks are the draw at this lively Spanish cafe-bar, along with budget wines and other drinks. There's usually a selection of nine different sandwiches at any given time (from a larger rotating menu), with toppings like crabmeat salad, salmon-cream cheese, Spanish tortilla and prosciutto.

If you want more variety you can choose from tapas-style dishes, paella and salads. Individual sandwiches start at ¥220, or ¥200 at lunchtime. Lizzeran is open from 8 am if you're in need of a quick Spanish-style breakfast.

Luke's Lobster (Harajuku)
Luke's（ルークスロブスター）

Lobster rolls—lobster meat on a toasted bun—are the specialty at this famous New York-based shop. All the lobsters come straight from Maine, and a display in front of the shop introduces their fisherman suppliers and identifies the lobster of the day.

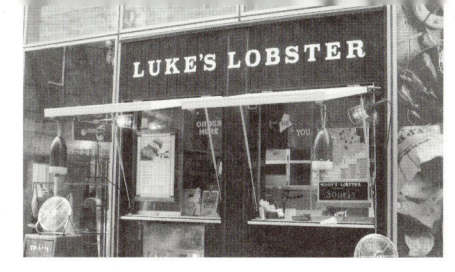

They also serve crab and shrimp sandwiches and combinations, but the lobster version seems to be the tastiest. Sandwiches are priced from ¥980, with optional chips and drinks. There's a small bench in front of the take-out window if you want to eat on-site.

Dominique Ansel Bakery Tokyo(Harajuku)
ドミニクアンセルベーカリー

Located down the street from Luke's, this New York-based French bakery offers a more upscale version of the lobster roll in their frilly second-floor "Petit Park" cafe. Fresh lobster tail meat on a lightly toasted, butter-soaked bun runs ¥1800 and includes a side of french fries.

Other exotic brunch-friendly sandwiches include the Brooklyn (sauteed kale, pickled carrots, fried shallots and poached egg), and the Nolita (fresh figs, ricotta cheese and honey on toast).

Dominique Ansel is probably best known as the inventor of the cronut, the croissant-doughnut combination that took New York by storm when it was first introduced. These are also available in the downstairs bakery, although they sell out quickly.

Mi Choripan (Yoyogi-Uehara)
ミ・チョリパン

Mi Choripan proudly serves up what they call "Argentinian Soul Food"—overstuffed chorizo-sausage sandwiches seasoned with chimichurri, a piquant sauce made from minced garlic, oregano and other herbs, olive oil and vinegar. The sandwiches are commonly sold from street stalls in Argentina and other parts of Latin America, and now here in Tokyo.

Sausages are grilled to order while you wait, after which you can add your choice of spicy sauces and garnishes—there are five sauces to pick from, and you can try a bit of each. The full-size sandwich with garnishes is ¥1100, or you can get a plain-sausage version to go for ¥750 if you want to do your own garnishing at home. The shop is colorfully decorated in a Latin American motif, while reggae plays on the sound system.

Kuumba du falafel (Shibuya)
クンバドゥファラフェル

Falafel—a Middle Eastern dish of deep-fried chickpea balls—is served here in traditional pita-bread sandwiches with lettuce and tomato, pickles and a tahini-based sauce. This tiny eight-seat cafe also serves hummus (a garlicky chickpea dip) and nice lentil soup. A half-size sandwich is ¥880, and a falafel platter is ¥1580.

Fermintxo Boca (Roppongi 1-chome)
フェルミンチョ ボカ

Alluring Basque-style bocadillo baguette sandwiches are served at lunchtime here, and the namesake Fermintxo Boca sandwich (grilled Iberico pork loin, mozzarella and pimento) is especially recommended, as is the Iberico-pork sausage variety.

In the evenings the menu expands to include an array of tapas and drinks. Budget around ¥6000 at night, ¥1000–1500 during the day.

Data

Banh Mi Sandwich (Takadanobaba)
03-5937-4547
バインミーサンドイッチ
Takadanobaba 4-9-18, Shinjuku-ku
Open 11am-7pm (Sat -6pm). Closed Sundays, Mondays.

Cafe Hai (Kiyosumi-Shirakawa)
03-5620-5962
カフェ ハイ
Museum of Contemporary Art Tokyo 2F, Miyoshi 4-1-1, Koto-ku
Open 11am-5:30pm (LO). Closed Mondays.

Lizarran (Akasaka)
03-5572-7303
リザラン
Akasaka 3-2-6, Minato-ku
Open 8am-2pm, 5-10:30pm (LO) daily.

Luke's Lobster (Harajuku)
03-5778-3747
Luke's（ルークスロブスター）
Jingumae 6-7-1, Shibuya-ku
Open 11am-8pm daily.

Dominique Ansel Bakery Tokyo (Harajuku)
03-3486-1329
ドミニクアンセルベーカリー
Jingumae 5-7-14, Shibuya-ku
Open 8am-7pm daily.

Mi Choripan (Yoyogi-Uehara)
03-5790-9300
ミ・チョリパン
Uehara 2-4-8, Shibuya-ku
Open 11am-10pm (Mon 11-8). Closed Tue, 2nd, 4th Mon.

Kuumba du falafel (Shibuya)
03-6416-8396
クンバドゥファラフェル
Shinsencho 23-1, Shibuya-ku
Open 11:30am-2:30, 5:30-8:30pm (LO; Sun -6). Closed Mondays.

Fermintxo Boca (Roppongi 1-chome)
03-6426-5760
フェルミンチョ ボカ
Ark Hills South Tower 1F, Roppongi 1-4-5, Minato-ku
Open 11am-3, 5-10pm (LO; Sat -9pm). Closed Sundays, holidays.

Chapter 4

Casual and takeaway

軽食・お持ち帰りもできます

Online Map
bento.com/maps/casual.html

Gyōza

(pork dumplings)

餃子

Tasty, thick-skinned, pork-filled gyoza dumplings—you can order them in ramen shops as a side dish for your noodles, at izakaya-style pubs to accompany your drinks, and at convenience stores ready to take home, but generally the best dumplings in town are found in shops that specialize in this dish.

Gyoza dumplings are typically stuffed with a mixture of minced pork and finely chopped vegetables such as cabbage, and seasoned with garlic, ginger and spices. The thick, chewy casing holds everything together while the dumplings are deep-fried. Sometimes shops offer optional extra ingredients, such as shiso leaves, chives or extra garlic. Dumplings that are boiled rather than fried, called "sui-gyoza," are a popular alternative.

Many shops will let you order dumplings as part of a set meal with soup and either fried rice or white rice, as well as a la carte. In either event, when your dumplings arrive, use one of the tiny condiment dishes at your table to custom-blend your own dipping sauce, mixing soy sauce, vinegar and hot-pepper oil in proportions to suit your taste.

Vocabulary

gyōza	餃子・ぎょうざ	gyoza dumplings
yaki gyōza	焼餃子	fried gyoza dumplings
sui gyōza	水餃子	boiled gyoza dumplings
nira	にら・韮	chives
ninniku	にんにく・ニンニク	garlic
shiso	しそ	shiso (perilla) leaf
teishoku	定食	set meal

Kanda Gyōzaya Honten (Jimbocho)
神田餃子屋 本店

This bustling dumpling emporium serves eight varieties of gyoza, along with Chinese noodles and assorted stir-fry dishes. Large-size kurobuta (Berkshire pork) gyoza are the signature item here, with a meaty filling that's studded with crunchy cabbage and encased in a firm, chewy, lightly charred thick skin.

The miso-negi gyoza are smaller, with a similar chewy casing that's smothered in pungent scallions and a light miso-sesame dressing. Other variations include two kinds of sui-gyoza (one served in soup), crunchy "paripari" gyoza, oversized shrimp gyoza and shiso gyoza.

Gyoza come either a la carte, in a set meal with rice and soup, or with a half-size portion of fried rice, with prices starting around ¥620 for a la carte.

Okei (Iidabashi)
おけ以

There's just one style of gyoza at this unpretentious Chinese noodle shop, and they've been preparing it the same way for five decades now, with good-quality minced pork, chives, bok choy and seasoning, but no garlic.

The gyoza are crunchy on the bottom with an otherwise doughy casing and a very juicy and flavorful filling. Six pieces are priced at ¥600, and you can order two plates if you're hungry.

The menu also offers Chinese-style tantanmen noodles, with inexpensive stir-fries and other simple dishes in the evening. The drinks list features beer, Korean makkoli and whiskey-based highball cocktails.

Namja Gyōza Stadium (Ikebukuro)
ナンジャ餃子スタジアム

If you want to try a lot of different gyoza in one sitting, this is the place to be. Around a dozen famous gyoza shops from around the country are gathered here in this unusual theme park, located inside the very noisy Namja Town game center. (Note that weekdays tend to be quieter than weekends.)

Portions are on the small side, so you can try a few different styles, choosing from the picture menus at each stall. When you're ready for dessert, next to the gyoza zone is a shop called Ice Parlor where you'll find fifty flavors of ice cream, including odd ones like basil, beef tongue, Indian curry and crabmeat.

Note that in order to access the gyoza area you'll have to pay an admission fee of ¥500 to get into Namja Town; think of it as a cover charge.

Pairon (Iidabashi)
白龍（パイロン）

The dumplings at this small specialty shop incorporate a more Chinese-tasting mix of spices and ingredients than is typical for Tokyo gyoza. The namesake Pairon ("white dragon") gyoza are small and lozenge-shaped, with a sweetish, mushy filling and a hint of cinnamon in the chewy skin. The thin, rectangular shiso gyoza have a firmer, very savory pork filling and big shiso leaves.

There are several other gyoza variations, plus dim sum dishes like daikon mochi and shrimp with mayonnaise. The a la carte menu is more limited at lunchtime, but you can order lunch specials that include rice and soup and side dishes alongside your dumplings.

Tiger Gyōza Hall (Asakusa)
タイガー餃子会舘 浅草別舘

Run by a large and diverse Asian-cuisine restaurant group, Tiger is devoted solely to gyoza dumplings, both fried and boiled. The signature dish is the extra-large Banana Gyoza, so named for its elongated shape. These have a voluminous pork filling that's wrapped in a thick, chewy, lightly charred casing.

Also worth checking out are the boiled dumplings (sui-gyoza), filled with an interesting mix of pork and chopped greens and wrapped in a green-colored handmade casing. Dumpings are served a la carte or as part of a set meal with rice, soup and pickles; budget around ¥1000 for a meal.

Harajuku Gyōza Lou (Harajuku)
原宿餃子樓

With its large wrap-around counter as well as a row of booths along the side, Lou is much bigger than your average gyoza shop, and it seems like one of the cooler places in town to satisfy your dumpling requirements. They're open until the first train of the morning every night but Sunday, making this a good place to stop in for a tasty snack when you've been out on the town.

Both fried and boiled gyoza will run you ¥290 for a set of six small dumplings. Each type comes in a regular version and a version with extra garlic and nira (chives)—the latter is recommended, or you can try them both to compare. Freshly prepared to order, the fried gyoza are decidedly ungreasy, with a casing that's soft rather than chewy.

Note that there's no English signage on the shop, but this is the only dumpling shop in the area, and one of the few places open at 4 am.

More gyōza

- **Fujitohachi,** listed in the Regional specialties chapter (page 81), serves a local variation of gyoza that's popular in the city of Hamamatsu, in Shizuoka Prefecture.

Data

Kanda Gyōzaya Honten (Jimbocho) — 03-3292-5965
神田餃子屋 本店
Kanda Jimbocho 1-4, Chiyoda-ku
Open 11am-10:15pm (LO; Sa, Su -9:30) daily.

Okei (Iidabashi) — 03-3261-3930
おけ以
Fujimi 2-12-16, Chiyoda-ku
Open 11:30am-1:50, 5-8:50pm (LO). Closed Sun, 3rd Sat.

Namja Gyōza Stadium (Ikebukuro) — 03-5950-0765
ナンジャ餃子スタジアム
Sunshine City World Import Mart 2F, Higashi-Ikebukuro 3-1-2, Toshima-ku
Open 10am-10pm daily.

Pairon (Iidabashi) — 03-3260-6571
白龍
Shin-Ogawacho 8-32, Shinjuku-ku
Open 11:30am-11:30pm. Closed Saturdays.

Tiger Gyōza Hall (Asakusa) — 03-3847-1355
タイガー餃子会舘 浅草別舘
Asakusa 1-25-17, Taito-ku
Open 11:30am-10:30pm (LO) daily.

Harajuku Gyōza Lou (Harajuku) — 03-3406-4743
原宿餃子樓
Jingumae 6-2-4, Shibuya-ku
Open 11:30am-4:30am (Su -10pm) daily.

Takoyaki and Akashiyaki

(octopus dumplings)

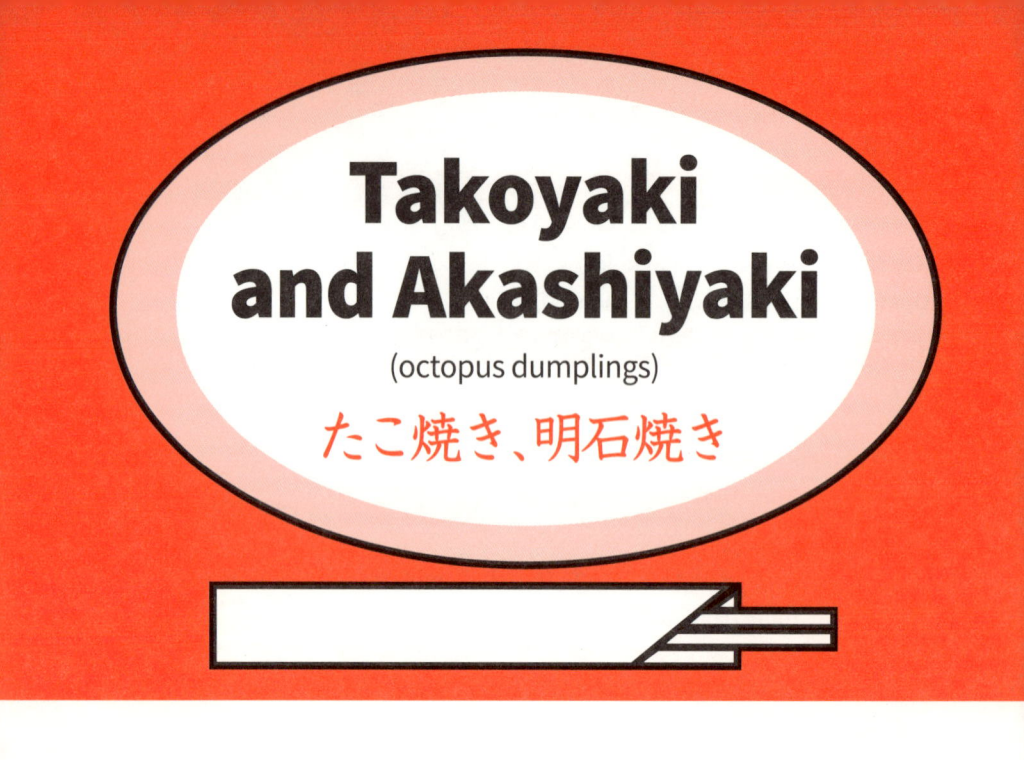

たこ焼き、明石焼き

Takoyaki, or grilled octopus dumplings, are a beloved snack food of the Osaka area. They're made by adding chopped-up bits of boiled octopus to a batter, then cooking over a special grill with hemispherical indentations. In Tokyo, takoyaki can be found in inexpensive, informal after-work bars and in take-out stands and retail stalls, some of them furnished with tables for in-store eating.

Takoyaki Museum, a takoyaki-themed food court in the Odaiba area of Tokyo, is a collection of five different takoyaki shops in one location, and it's a fun spot to try out different types of takoyaki without traveling all over town. Elsewhere, takoyaki sellers can be recognized by their distinctively shaped grills, usually placed in the front window of a shop.

Takoyaki shops offer various combinations of toppings and condiments, such as custom-made spicy sauces, flavored mayonnaise, chopped scallions, cheese and so on.

Often you can order an assorted platter to compare several different toppings. The texture of the dumplings themselves can also vary from shop to shop—some places turn out a crunchy outer shell, while others favor a more elastic skin.

Akashiyaki, another type of octopus dumpling, is a specialty of the city of Akashi, located west of Kobe and alongside the octopus-fishing waters of the Akashi Strait. It's similar in preparation to takoyaki, but incorporates egg in the batter, resulting in a dumpling with a light and spongy texture and a more omelette-like flavor. It's served with a mild broth in which to dip the dumplings before eating.

A few of the shops listed in this section serve both akashiyaki and takoyaki. All shops have take-out service.

Vocabulary

takoyaki　たこ焼き　octopus dumpling

akashiyaki　明石焼き　octopus egg dumpling

sōsu　ソース　spicy takoyaki sauce

negi　ネギ・葱　scallions

chiizu　チーズ　cheese

mayo(nēzu)　マヨ（ネーズ）　mayonnaise

mentaiko mayonēzu　明太子マヨネーズ　spicy cod-roe mayonnaise

shio　塩　salt

ponzu　ポン酢　vinegar-soy dip

dashi　だし　broth for dipping

biiru　ビール　beer

haibōru　ハイボール　"highball" cocktail

Creoru (Shibuya)
くれおーる 道玄坂1丁目店

Takoyaki, yakisoba and kushiage are served at this late-night, Osaka-based bar. In addition to more orthodox toppings, Creoru offers fun takoyaki variations like truffle oil, ume-shiso, and anchovy mayonnaise with black olives. Especially recommended is the tasty pepperoncino takoyaki, topped with toasted garlic chips, red pepper and a bit of salt.

All the takoyaki dumplings are brimming with bigger-than-average chunks of octopus, in a filling that's halfway between creamy and fluffy, with just a thin outer skin. The menu also features "Osaka-style drinks," which means frozen plum liquor and various highball cocktails as well as red and white wines.

There's a tiny six-seat counter on the ground floor along with a busy grill in the front take-out window; upstairs there's space for another twenty or so customers. Menus are bilingual.

Kukuru (Daiba)
たこ家 道頓堀 くくる

My favorite of the shops inside the Takoyaki Museum mini-theme park, Kukuru offers three takoyaki variations—regular, cheese, and akashiyaki.

The regular version has nicely balanced flavors and tasty octopus bits, while the omelette base of the akashiyaki is pleasantly runny and soft. A set of four regular and four akashiyaki is ¥630, and a sampler of all three types is ¥980. An English menu is available.

Osaka Hyakkaten (Yurakucho)
大阪百貨店

The standing bar corner of Osaka's antenna shop is surprisingly lively in the evenings, when neighborhood office workers and passersby drop in for inexpensive drinks and snacks. This is a comfortable place to sample takoyaki dumplings, although it may take several minutes before your order is ready.

The dumplings are wrapped in a slightly elastic coating that's filled with a creamy batter and tender chunks of octopus. You can order them with yuzudashi (citrus-flavored dipping broth) if you want a fresher-tasting alternative to the usual sauce and mayonnaise topping. They also serve Chinese-style steamed pork buns, cocktails and beer.

Juhachiban (Daiba)
たこ焼 十八番

Juhachiban set themselves apart from the other shops in Daiba's takoyaki theme park with their pleasantly crunchy shell, made by using harder-than-average tenkasu (bits of tempura-fried batter) in the takoyaki batter. Among the variations here is a simple salt and toasted nori version that really brings out the flavor of the octopus filling.

The regular version is also quite nice, with a slightly tart sauce. Sampler sets of two, three and four types of takoyaki are available; a three-part assortment is ¥840. English menus are provided.

Minatoya (Sasazuka)
みなと屋

This charming neighborhood shop serves takoyaki, akashi-yaki, octopus-filled okonomi-yaki pancakes, and kakigori shaved-ice desserts. The takoyaki is a fairly orthodox version, studded with big, tasty chunks of octopus in a gooey filling. It's served on its own or in a snack called takosen, which is two takoyaki balls in a crunchy shrimp-cracker sandwich.

The egg-based akashiyaki dumplings come plain or in a version that incorporates fresh-tasting leek alongside the octopus. During the day, plump kakigori shaved-ice balls seem to be the biggest draw here. These come in interesting variations like avocado-milk and strawberry-pistachio, with an ever-changing roster of flavors.

Akashiyaki with leek is ¥690 for eight pieces, okonomiyaki with cabbage is ¥450, and a takosen snack is ¥180.

Tennoji Hachihachi (Otsuka)
天王寺 はち八

Akashiyaki, takoyaki and Kansai-style oden are the mainstays at this very down-to-earth drinking spot, which is the Tokyo outpost of an Osaka-based shop. The akashiyaki has a soft and slightly runny consistency, and it tends to fall apart as you eat it. It's served here with red pepper, Sichuan-style sansho pepper, scallions and pickled ginger, plus an aromatic hot dipping broth.

Akashiyaki are ¥780 for eight pieces, and a bowl of assorted oden is ¥880. Cocktails are priced in the ¥390–450 range, and regular customers can order a bottle of cheap shochu and have their name marked on the side of the bottle for subsequent visits. There's an eleven-seat counter and a few small tables in back.

Donaiya (Otsuka)
元祖どないや アトレヴィ大塚店

　The takoyaki here embodies a dramatic contrast of textures—a firm and slightly chewy outer shell surrounding an interior that's squishy and gooey, ready to come gushing out when prodded with chopsticks. The octopus, when you can find a piece, is remarkably soft and tender. Mentaiko (codfish roe) mayonnaise sauce is an appealingly spicy topping, and worth the ¥50 extra; other options include tart ponzu sauce, dashi, soy sauce and plain salt.

　There are eight takoyaki variations in all, starting at ¥450 for a plate of six, or you can spring for the ¥980 twelve-piece platter which lets you try four different toppings. The shop also serves yakisoba and several types of udon noodles as well as beer and cheap cocktails (from ¥320).

Located inside the ground-floor food hall of the Atre mall in Otsuka station, Donaiya has twelve seats and also does take-out service. As usual for Tokyo takoyaki shops, the main branch is located in Osaka.

Data

Creoru (Shibuya) — 03-5459-2100
くれおーる 道玄坂1丁目店
Dogenzaka 1-6-4, Shibuya-ku
Open 5pm-4am (Sun -midnight) daily.

Kukuru (Daiba) — 03-3599-6017
たこ家 道頓堀 くくる
Decks Tokyo Beach Seaside Mall 4F, Daiba 1-6-1, Minato-ku
Open 11am-9pm daily.

Osaka Hyakkaten (Yurakucho) — 03-5220-1333
大阪百貨店
Tokyo Kotsu Kaikan 1F, Yurakucho 2-10-1, Chiyoda-ku
Open 10am-10pm daily.

Juhachiban (Daiba) — 03-3599-6218
たこ焼 十八番
Decks Tokyo Beach Seaside Mall 4F, Daiba 1-6-1, Minato-ku
Open 11am-9pm daily.

Minatoya (Sasazuka) — 03-6383-3120
みなと屋
Sasazuka 2-41-20, Shibuya-ku
Open 11am-9pm. Closed Wednesdays.

Tennoji Hachihachi (Otsuka) — 03-3590-5688
天王寺 はち八
Minami-Otsuka 3-53-3, Toshima-ku
Open 11:30am-midnight daily.

Donaiya (Otsuka) — 03-3984-5115
元祖どないや アトレヴィ大塚店
Atre Vie Otsuka 1F, Minami-Otsuka 3-33-1, Toshima-ku
Open 10am-9pm daily.

Chicken karaage

(deep-fried chicken)

鶏の唐揚げ

Tori karaage is Japanese-style fried chicken, beloved by Japanese children and adults and a staple item at izakaya, school cafeterias, family restaurants and convenience stores. It's prepared by marinating bite-size pieces of chicken, then dredging them in flour and/or corn-starch and deep-frying them to a golden brown.

While you can find tasty karaage at many izakaya, some of the best chicken comes from small counter shops and take-out stands around Tokyo that specialize in this one dish. Specialty shops generally fry up your chicken after you've made your order, although there may be trays of pre-cooked chicken ready to go for customers in a hurry.

Chicken karaage

Chapter 4 Casual and takeaway

Vocabulary

karaage 唐揚・からあげ deep-fried (chicken) without batter
momo もも chicken thigh meat
sasami 笹身・ささみ chicken breast meat
teba 手羽 chicken wing
kawa 皮・かわ chicken skin
bonchiri ぼんちり fatty chicken tail
seseri せせり chicken neck meat
rebā レバー liver
sunagimo 砂肝 gizzard
hatsu はつ・ハツ heart

Tokyo Karaage Bar (Marunouchi)
東京から揚げバル

Tokyo Karaage Bar does more than just serve great fried chicken—they've turned it into a fun evening out. The menu is much more elaborate than other karaage shops: first of all, you get to choose your favorite parts of the bird—wings, breast, thigh, fatty bonjiri (tail), gizzards, liver. Each order is around ¥378, so you can mix and match without worrying too much about the evening's budget.

You can also customize your chicken with a dozen different dips (or "toppings" as they're called here). These come in flavors like shallot tartar sauce, classic yuzu kosho, and an ultra-spicy "death salsa." The freshly fried chicken is impressively crisp on the outside, with a satisfying crunch and juicy, tender meat.

Drinks include wine and cocktails as well as beer, and starters like smoked duck and pork rillettes can round out your meal if you want to get fancy. The setting is very casual and lively—a counter surrounding the kitchen, plus a few barrel-tables up front with stools.

Torian (Hatagaya)
とりあん 幡ヶ谷店

Mostly a local neighborhood take-out joint, Torian also provides a few seats if you want to eat here. The chicken is on the juicy end of the scale and nicely seasoned; variations include nankotsu (cartilage) and gizzards as well as thigh meat.

Karayama (Shimbashi)
からやま 新橋店

While many serious karaage shops will custom-fry each order, Karayama has a big enough turnover that they can often serve you an order of hot, freshly fried chicken just seconds after you sit down. Most menu items are either teishoku or bento set meals, with rice and soup, but if you look carefully at the ticket machine you can find the buttons to order chicken by the piece.

The regular karaage comes in large pieces (¥130 each) that are dark gold in color, quite juicy inside with a moderately crisp skin. There's also a mildly ginger-infused option (¥150 per piece) if you want some variety. A sweet sesame sauce is available for dipping, although I would have preferred something spicier. Take-out is available if you want to spice things up on your own, or you can sit at the family-restaurant-style twenty-seat counter.

Gaburi Chicken (Akasaka)
がブリチキン。赤坂店

With numerous branches all over Tokyo, this Nagoya-based fried-chicken chain must be doing something right. Their chicken is definitely on the oily end of the spectrum, more juicy than crisp, and fried up fresh with each order. You can choose from six different cuts of meat, with options like chicken neck meat, wings, and "yagen" (breast meat with cartilage), along with several different optional dipping sauces like yuzu-kosho and ume (plum).

There's an inexpensive wine list in addition to the usual cocktails and beer. Overall the atmosphere tends to be lively and festive, and they're open quite late. Budget around ¥1500–2000 for dinner with drinks.

Moriyama (Gakugeidaigaku-mae)
もり山 学芸大学店

Special blended spices, ginger and home-cultivated garlic are some of the flavor secrets of the fried chicken here, and several different cuts of chicken are available to choose from. This small neighborhood take-out shop is the only Tokyo branch of a popular Kyushu-based chain.

Yukari (Asakusa)
からあげ 縁 浅草総本店

This highly regarded take-out-only shop offers extra-crispy and extra-juicy options, as well as a garlic-packed version. You can also choose chicken wings, nankotsu (chicken with crunchy cartilage) and fried and pounded chicken skin. The extra-crispy version indeed does have a very satisfying crunch, even after you get it home.

Data

Tokyo Karaage Bar (Marunouchi) — 03-6256-0564
東京から揚げバル
JP Tower Kitte B1F, Marunouchi 2-7-2, Chiyoda-ku
Open 10am-9pm (LO) daily.

Torian (Hatagaya) — 03-5351-1755
とりあん 幡ヶ谷店
Hatagaya 2-8-9, Shibuya-ku
Open 11:30am-2, 4:30-midnight. Closed 1st, 3rd Wed.

Karayama (Shimbashi) — 03-3519-7997
からやま 新橋店
New Shimbashi Bldg 1F, Shimbashi 2-16-11, Minato-ku
Open 10:30am-10pm (LO). Closed 2nd Sunday.

Gaburi Chicken (Akasaka) — 03-6441-2330
がブリチキン。赤坂店
Akasaka 3-17-7, Minato-ku
Open 5pm-5am daily.

Moriyama (Gakugeidaigaku-mae) — 03-3719-5730
もり山 学芸大学店
Takaban 2-8-21, Meguro-ku
Open 11am-7:45pm (LO) daily.

Yukari (Asakusa) — 03-3845-3433
からあげ 縁 浅草総本店
Asakusa 1-24-7, Taito-ku
Open 10am-10pm daily.

Chicken karaage

Chapter 4 Casual and takeaway

Kakigōri

(shaved-ice desserts)

かき氷

Kakigori is Japanese shaved ice. If you are expecting carnival-style crushed ice cubes topped with sickly-sweet rainbow colors, guess again. Japanese kakigori aims to be as fuwa-fuwa (fluffy and cloud-like) as possible, with fresh toppings that accentuate the seasons. Expensive machines shave a block of ice razor-thin. The better shops even import their water from fresh springs in the mountains of the countryside.

Though it is often enjoyed in the hot summer months, some kakigori shops, especially those in the older neighborhoods of Tokyo, stay open year round.

Common toppings include:
- fresh strawberry, peach, or mango; often accentuated with sweetened milk
- matcha (green tea) and azuki (sweet red beans)
- fresh Japanese citrus sweetened with honey and ginger
- chestnut and pumpkin cream
- kuromitsu (black sugar syrup) with mochi (small rice cakes)

Shimura (Mejiro)
志むら

The kakigori at Shimura can be ordered on the second floor, above the traditional sweets shop that has been in the area for many, many years. Their kakigori menu features all the usual suspects, with the fresh strawberry being the most popular. Be sure to order it made with natural spring water from Yatsugatake in the Southern Alps of Japan. For only an extra ¥100, you get some of the cleanest water in the country. The strawberries are only slightly sweetened, meaning this massive serving of kakigori is surprisingly easy to eat.

Himitsudo (Nippori)
ひみつ堂

Himitsudo is located in a charming part of Tokyo's north side—Yanaka Ginza. This old-world shopping street, only a few minutes walk from Nippori Station, is a great place to spend an hour or two. Himitsudo, even though its location feels like a secret, is one of Tokyo's most revered kakigori shops. They pride themselves on a constantly changing menu, and boast the use of 132 secret toppings. Even regulars are surprised by some of their choices, like the Japanese pumpkin and caramel. Prices vary from ¥700–900.

Darumaya (Kita-ku)
だるまや餅菓子店

Darumaya lies along the Jujo Ginza Shotengai, a covered shopping street in northern Tokyo. Despite its location off the beaten track, this old-world cafe serves some of the city's most popular kakigori. The master is an encyclopedia of food knowledge, especially when it comes to tea and coffee. The green tea and azuki bean kakigori is particularly nice, but for something different try the special coffee kakigori (¥1100), or go for their ultra-high-class version (¥2600).

Soranoiro Salt and Mushroom (Kojimachi)
ソラノイロ ソルトアンドマッシュルーム

Kakigori at a ramen shop? In recent years, a few ramen shops have started selling kakigori on the side. One of the best, for both ramen and kakigori, is Soranoiro's second shop, called Salt and Mushroom. From 1 pm, you can get their unique kakigori, made out of blocks of ice containing milk and cream. Fresh fruit toppings are the norm, with strawberries from Hokkaido being a popular choice. Be sure to check out their daily seasonal fruit choice as well. [On holidays they're open only for lunch.]

Data

Shimura (Mejiro)   03-3953-3388
志むら
Mejiro 3-13-3, Toshima-ku
Open 10am-6:30pm (LO). Closed Sundays.

Himitsudo (Nippori)   03-3824-4132
ひみつ堂
Yanaka 3-11-18, Taito-ku
Open 11am-8pm (Sat, Sun 10am-). Closed Mondays.

Darumaya (Kita-ku)   03-3908-6644
だるまや餅菓子店
Jujo Nakahara 1-3-6, Kita-ku
Open 10:30am-6:30pm (LO). Closed Tuesdays.

Soranoiro Salt and Mushroom (Kojimachi)   03-6272-6886
ソラノイロ ソルトアンドマッシュルーム
Kojimachi 3-4-3, Chiyoda-ku
Open 11am-3, 6-10:20pm (LO). Closed Saturdays, Sundays.

Regional "antenna shops" and more takeaway

地方特産品
アンテナショップ

One of the joys of traveling around Japan, for both Japanese and foreign visitors, is trying out various local cuisines and special local dishes. To encourage tourism and to show off the best of their local products, the governments of prefectures around Japan have set up so-called "antenna shops" in Tokyo.

These retail shops sell fresh produce, pickled vegetables, frozen seafood, packaged fish cakes and crackers, and small-producer soy sauce and miso from their various prefectures. They also carry sake, shochu, fruit liqueurs and craft beers, as well as pottery and other handicrafts. In addition to promoting travel, they supply transplanted natives of far-off prefectures with a chance to buy familiar local products and enjoy the flavors of their hometowns.

I've mentioned a few antenna shops already in the chapter on regional cuisines, but here I'll introduce some prefectural antenna shops that sell appealing local dishes to take home. And while there isn't really space to cover the many sources of excellent take-out food in Tokyo, such as the vast food halls located in the basements of department stores, I will introduce a few stand-alone shops with great B-kyu style snacks to go.

Vocabulary

antenna shoppu　アンテナショップ　"antenna shop"
bentō　弁当　bento box
korokke　コロッケ　croquettes
shūmai　シュウマイ　Chinese-style shumai dumplings
satsuma-age　さつま揚げ　deep-fried fish cakes
senbei　せんべい　savory grilled crackers
dango　団子・だんご　(mochi) sweet dumplings

Ekibenya Matsuri (Yaesu)
駅弁屋 祭

Eki-ben—bento boxes sold at train stations that are built around regional dishes or special local ingredients—have a long tradition in Japan. Celebrating that tradition, this very popular shop inside Tokyo station sells an astonishing 170 different eki-ben from various stations throughout Japan—all freshly prepared.

    For those who have trouble choosing, the shop lists the top-ranked bento by popularity. Grilled Yonezawa beef from Yamagata, seafood omelettes from Niigata, and beef tongue from Sendai are at the top of the list.

Kagoshima Yuraku-Kan (Hibiya)
かごしま遊楽館

Among Tokyo's many prefectural antenna shops, this Kagoshima (Kyushu) shop probably has the biggest selection of freshly prepared foods ready to go. At the take-out deli counter you'll find a wide assortment of satsuma-age, deep-fried fish cakes and vegetable fritters that are a popular local snack. Explore the rest of the shop for frozen Berkshire-pork stews, frozen fish, vacuum-packed charcoal-grilled chicken, plenty of pickles, fresh yams, and a huge selection of shochu.

Hokkaido Dosanko Plaza (Yurakucho)
北海道どさんこプラザ 有楽町店

Hokkaido is well known for its potatoes, and this popular antenna shop does a brisk take-out trade in freshly made potato croquettes, both plain and with beef. Another big draw is their dumpling counter, where you'll find Hokkaido-style crab shumai dumplings and tako zangi (octopus dumplings) to take away. Occasionally they give out samples so you can try before you buy. Packaged foods include ice cream, cheese and other dairy products, limited-edition chocolates, soup curry, tomato juice and a good selection of Hokkaido wines.

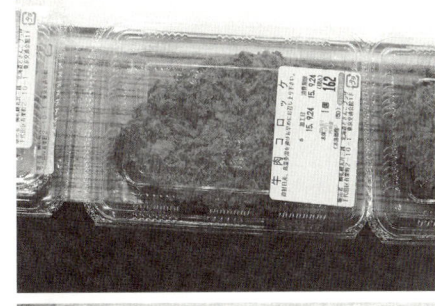

Ichibanya (Asakusa)
壱番屋

There are many places around town where you can buy sembei crackers, but Ichibanya is the most entertaining. Here you can choose from over a hundred varieties, with exotic flavors like wasabi, hot pepper, shiso, plum, garlic, and seaweed. There are surprises like spicy cod roe and bonito, mysterious "salad" flavors, and shiso with sweet icing.

Pick up a basket at the door and fill it up as your browse the selection—everything is quite reasonably priced. Gift-pack assortments of the most popular flavors are available if you have trouble deciding. On your way out you can admire the skills of the chef roasting fresh sembei at the charcoal grill in the front window.

Midette (Mitsukoshimae)
日本橋ふくしま館Midette

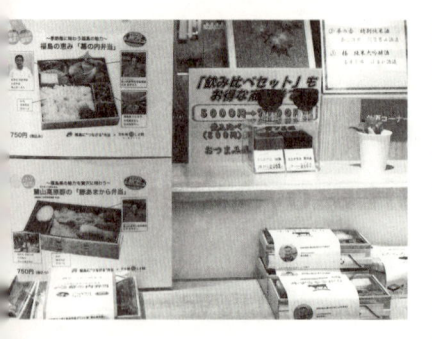

Besides the usual produce, sake and handicrafts, this Fukushima antenna shop offers four different bento lunches at midday, to take out or to eat at the small counter area; free tea is provided. The varieties are beef, pork, tuna, and a maku-no-uchi (house special), and they're priced at around ¥750 each. From 4:00–7:30 pm the same counter turns into a bar, offering three-part sake tastings of premium Fukushima sake for around ¥500.

Iwate Ginga Plaza (Higashi-Ginza)
いわて銀河プラザ

This sprawling prefectural specialty shop sells everything from crabmeat, uni and ikura bento boxes at the front entrance, to mochi pounded-rice dumplings, Iwate beef and dairy products. There's a respectable sake selection as well as craft beers from three different local breweries (Zumona, Baeren, and Iwate Kura).
[Note that the shop closes early, at 5 pm, on the last day of the month.]

Imahan Sozai (Ningyocho)
今半惣菜

Run by Imahan, a century-old sukiyaki and shabu-shabu restaurant, this popular take-out counter is located across the alleyway from their flagship restaurant. While a sukiyaki dinner at the restaurant might run you

¥5000, here you can grab some take-out sukiyaki-filled croquettes for just ¥173, and sukiyaki nikuman (Chinese pork buns) for ¥626.

There's a whole range of deep-fried fare for your dining pleasure—chicken karaage, corn-cream croquettes, lotus root stuffed with ground pork, and deep-fried oysters, prawns, squid and mackerel. They also sell premium-brand roast pork and a variety of salad-type dishes. Party-ready hors d'oeuvre platters are ¥3240 for a 3–4 person party.

Yabaton Kitte Granche (Marunouchi)
矢場とん キッテグランシェ店

Yabaton is Nagoya's most popular tonkatsu shop, and this small take-out stand offers not just tonkatsu but also a good selection of inexpensive kushiage and other deep-fried fare. Choose your own selection from kushi-katsu (basic deep-fried pork on skewers), pork with basil and cheese, crunchy pork-stuffed lotus root, pork cutlet with big chunks of leek, and spicy mentaiko (cod or pollock roe) with oba leaf.

Everything you order comes with Yabaton's signature miso-based sauce on the side. If you can't wait to bring it home, you can grab a table and stool in the rather bare-bones dining area and eat there—let them know so they can heat up your order. Individual skewers start from around ¥162. (Located inside the Kitte Granche area in the basement of JP Tower.)

More antenna-shop adventures

- **Konne** (新宿宮崎館 KONNE), an antenna shop for Miyazaki Prefecture in Kyushu, serves freshly made charcoal-grilled chicken in their cafeteria corner, and also sells vacuum-packed pouches to take home. See page 80 for details.
- **Osaka Hyakkaten** (大阪百貨店), an antenna shop for Osaka Prefecture, has a lively standing-bar corner where they serve freshly made takoyaki to eat in or take out. See page 208 in the Takoyaki chapter for details.
- **Sanshou** (三匠) okonomiyaki restaurant is located inside the Hiroshima Prefecture antenna shop in Ginza. See page 109 of the Okonomiyaki chapter for details.

Data

Ekibenya Matsuri (Yaesu) — 03-3213-4352
駅弁屋 祭
Tokyo Station Central Street 1F, Marunouchi 1-9-1, Chiyoda-ku
Open 5:30am-11pm daily.

Kagoshima Yuraku-Kan (Hibiya) — 03-3506-9177
かごしま遊楽館
Chiyoda Bldg 1-3F, 9F, Yurakucho 1-6-4, Chiyoda-ku
Open 10am-8pm (Sat, Sun -7pm) daily.

Hokkaido Dosanko Plaza (Yurakucho) — 03-5224-3800
北海道どさんこプラザ 有楽町店
Tokyo Kotsu Kaikan 1F, Yurakucho 2-10-1, Chiyoda-ku
Open 10am-8pm daily.

Ichibanya (Asakusa) — 03-3842-5001
壱番屋
Asakusa 1-32-8, Taito-ku
Open 9am-7pm daily.

Midette (Mitsukoshimae) — 03-6262-3977
日本橋ふくしま館Midette
Nihonbashi Muromachi 4-3-16, Chuo-ku
Open 11am-8pm (Sat, Sun -6pm) daily.

Iwate Ginga Plaza (Higashi-Ginza) — 03-3524-8282
いわて銀河プラザ
Ginza 5-15-1, Chuo-ku
Open 10:30am-7pm daily.

Imahan Sozai (Ningyocho) — 03-3666-1240
今半惣菜
Nihonbashi Ningyocho 2-9-14, Chuo-ku
Open 11am-7pm daily.

Yabaton Kitte Granche (Marunouchi) — 03-3211-8810
矢場とん キッテグランシェ店
JP Tower Kitte B1F, Marunouchi 2-7-2, Chiyoda-ku
Open 10am-9pm (Sun -8pm) daily.

Chapter 4 Casual and takeaway

Regional "antenna shops" and more takeaway

TOKYO BEYOND SUSHI
A guide to the backstreet eateries and
down-home comfort foods that
Tokyo people love

英文版 東京 B 級グルメガイド

2016 年 3 月 1 日　第 1 刷発行

著　者　　ロブ・サターホワイト

発行者　　浦　晋亮

発行所　　IBC パブリッシング株式会社
　　　　　〒 162-0804 東京都新宿区中里町 29 番 3 号 菱秀神楽坂ビル 9F
　　　　　Tel. 03-3513-4511 Fax. 03-3513-4512
　　　　　www.ibcpub.co.jp

印刷所　　株式会社シナノパブリッシングプレス

©Robb Satterwhite 2016
©IBC Publishing, Inc. 2016
Printed in Japan

落丁本・乱丁本は、小社宛にお送りください。送料小社負担にてお取り替えいたします。
本書の無断複写 (コピー) は著作権法上での例外を除き禁じられています。

ISBN978-4-7946-0401-9